# THE O BROTHEI

## WHEN FREEMASONRY CROSSED THE ENGLISH CHANNEL

Darren Lorente-Bull

First published 2018
Copyright © Darren Lorente-Bull
All rights reserved. No part of this book may be reproduced or transmitted in any form or by any means, electronic or mechanical, including, photocopying, recording, scanning or by any information storage and retrieval system, on the internet or elsewhere, without permission from the Publisher in writing.
Cover Design Mayu Omori
Illustrated by Manuel Martinez Brunete, Sergio Simancas & Mayu Omori

Picture Credits: Every effort has been made to identify and correctly attribute photographic credits. Should any error have occurred this is entirely unintentional.

Published by
**FALCON BOOKS PUBLISHING LTD**
WWW.FALCONBOOKSPUBLISING.COM

FALCON BOOKS
PUBLISHING
2018

Falcon Books Publishing: 71-75 Shelton Street Covent Garden, London WC2H 9JQ, England.

ISBN-13: 978-9869492560

ISBN-10: 9869492568

# THE OTHER BROTHERHOOD

## WHEN FREEMASONRY CROSSED THE ENGLISH CHANNEL

Darren Lorente-Bull

Falcon Books
Publishing

Dedicated to the memory of Manuel Martinez Brunete, Spanish artist and businessman and Bro. Kenneth Hunt, Master Mason.

# ACKNOWLEDGEMENTS

To my wife Mayu and my children Jessica and Josh for their love and encouragement.

To my parents and to my brother for never giving up on me.

To Sergio Simancas for his friendship and for his beautiful artwork and that of his father, Manuel Martinez Brunete, which he kindly allowed me to use in this book. Sergio Simancas was born in Barcelona in 1972, studied at the French Lyceum in Barcelona and completed his degree in Fine Arts in the Miguel Hernandez University of Elche in 2004. Sergio is a very experienced graphic designer, painter and sequential artist and more information on him can be found in his excellent website:

https://sergiosimancasilustracionycomic.com

To Julian Rees, writer, friend, mentor and Freemason member of Maa Kheru Lodge 975 and the triangle Tir N'An Oige 990 working under the auspices of the British Federation of Le Droit Humain.

To Javier Otaola, writer, friend, mentor, fellow Christian, Freemason and former president of CLIPSAS and member of the Grand Symbolic Lodge of Spain.

To Philippe Bodhuin, Past Master of the Lodge Freedom of Conscience working under the auspices of the Grand Orient of France in London for his invaluable contribution.

To Lorena Clara Marques, Freemason and member of the Spanish Federation of Le Droit Humain for formatting the book and indexing it as well as for her candid interview, input and friendship.

To my pals the three musketeers: David Garcia-Cooke, Rubén Baidez Legidos and Alberto Moreno, also known as Bro. Brown, for their friendship, comments and general input.

# CONTENTS

ACKNOWLEDGEMENTS .................................................................. 4

CONTENTS ........................................................................................ 6

INTRODUCTION .............................................................................. 8

CHAPTER 1: Seeking a Definition ................................................... 10

    What is Freemasonry? ................................................................... 10

    1. Anglo-Saxon Freemasonry ......................................................... 15

    2. Liberal or Continental Freemasonry ........................................... 15

CHAPTER 2: The Origins .................................................................. 17

    Where did Freemasonry come from? ............................................ 17

    The Operatives ............................................................................. 17

    The Ancient Charges .................................................................... 18

    The Transition from Operative Freemasonry to Speculative Freemasonry .......................................................... 22

    The United Grand Lodge of England ........................................... 24

    Basic Principles for Grand Lodge Recognition ............................ 25

CHAPTER 3: French Freemasonry .................................................... 29

    Some Early Fringe Orders ............................................................ 29

    French or Continental Freemasonry ............................................. 31

    Philosophical and Literary Influences .......................................... 33

    Mystical and Chivalric Influences ................................................ 39

    The French Revolution ................................................................. 40

CHAPTER 4: The Birth of Liberal Freemasonry..................44

    Le Grand Orient de France................................44

    Grande Loge de France......................................51

    Le Droit Humain................................................52

    Le Droit Humain in Great Britain....................54

CHAPTER 5: The uses of Freemasonry................................59

    Political Freemasonry........................................59

    Esoteric Freemasonry........................................61

    Philosophical Freemasonry................................63

CHAPTER 6: Universalism....................................................65

    The Appeal of Strasbourg..................................65

Listed Below are the Basic Principles Which CATENA Follow:........................................................70

CONCLUSION........................................................................72

ABOUT THE AUTHOR..........................................................78

APPENDIX 1............................................................................80

APPENDIX 2............................................................................88

APPENDIX 3............................................................................94

APPENDIX 4..........................................................................100

APPENDIX 5..........................................................................106

BIBLIOGRAPHY...................................................................114

ONLINE RESOURCES........................................................116

# INTRODUCTION

In this book, I will introduce the concept of Liberal Freemasonry to the English-speaking reader, who will perhaps be more accustomed to the mainstream, regular male-only version of Freemasonry.

In the United Kingdom, regular Freemasonry is part and parcel of the establishment; the Duke of Kent is its Grand Master. Lodges work to the Glory of the Great Architect of the Universe and discussion of political and religious matters is forbidden. The downside of this model of Freemasonry is that women and atheists are excluded from joining and any other model of Freemasonry which does not follow these landmarks, is not recognised as being 'regular.' This other model of Freemasonry does indeed exist and it is known as Liberal or Adogmatic Freemasonry and has been largely ignored in the English and American Masonic and esoteric literary traditions.

The largest Masonic Order in France, Le Grand Orient de France is one of the most important liberal or adogmatic Masonic Orders in the world. This is an Order which accepts women and atheists as members; it is also a Masonic Order which is not recognised by the United Grand Lodge of England or any of its American counterparts. Le Droit Humain, a Masonic Order created in 1893 with the main purpose of initiating men and women alongside each other has 30,000 members spread over 50 countries. The British Federation of Le Droit Humain was founded by theosophists at the beginning of the twentieth century and offers a richly esoteric Masonic practice in its lodges.

The first Masonic lodges in France were consecrated by exiled English Jacobites in the seventeenth century. British institutions and ideas were very popular during the seventeenth and eighteenth centuries and Freemasonry took root in France and many other European countries during this period.

It would be possible to speculate that the genesis of Liberal Freemasonry began around 1877. This is when Le Grand Orient de France began to accept atheists into its ranks and as a consequence ceased to be recognised by the United Grand Lodge of England. But perhaps the seeds of this new, modern form of Freemasonry had already been planted in the 1700s with what we will refer to as 'fringe' Freemasonry. Examples of fringe Freemasonry are the Memphis Misraim Rite created by the self-styled Count Cagliostro, the Rite of Strict Observance and the lodges of adoption which initiated women. Freemasonry developed very differently on the European continent and was exposed to the ideals of the Enlightenment during its genesis whereas regular, speculative English Freemasonry had originated at least a century prior to the advent of the Enlightenment in Renaissance England.

This book charts the transition from English so called regular Freemasonry to Liberal or Adogmatic Freemasonry in France and other European countries, its subsequent development and how liberal masonic organisations such as CLIPSAS and CATENA are doing for Liberal Freemasonry what the United Grand Lodge of England is doing for regular Freemasonry. *The Other Brotherhood* also features some exclusive interviews with members of Le Droit Humain, the Gran Logia Simbólica Española and Le Grand Orient de France.

# CHAPTER 1: Seeking a Definition

## What is Freemasonry?

Freemasonry is a fraternal society present in almost every nation on the globe which exists as such, officially, since 1717 and has its origins in England. What differentiates Freemasonry from other fraternal and charitable societies such as the Rotaries or the Lions Club is the fact that Freemasonry makes use of ritual ceremonies to impart complex moral and philosophical teachings to its members. Freemasonry also differs from other organisations in one important respect: it has helped shape the modern world, at least in the west.

Freemasonry is many different things to different people. For some it is a fraternity dedicated to charitable works, for others a spiritual path. Some see Freemasonry as a philosophical Athenaeum and yet for others Freemasonry is a social and even a political instrument. The emphasis varies from country to country and even from lodge to lodge but what unites all without distinction is the fact that Freemasonry makes use of ritual to impart its teachings.

To summarise Freemasonry in one line, it is fitting to offer the description given of it in the old Emulation Ritual which in turn has its roots in the *Ahiman Rezon* manual:

*A system of morality veiled in allegory and illustrated by symbols.*

Of course, the scope of Freemasonry has the potential to go beyond that definition, but if I were to look for a global, universal definition I would stay with that one.

Freemasonry communicates its teachings through ritual dramas. We could make an analogy between Masonic ritual and the Ancient Mystery religions to try and explain what these ritual dramas are. The Ancient Mysteries were initiatory ceremonies which took place in Ancient Greece, Rome, Egypt and other parts of the classical world. In these mysteries, through the use of music and ritual ceremony is employed to raise the level of consciousness and spiritual awareness of the participants, in order to attain a higher consciousness.

There is no denying that a strong resemblance exists between the symbolism and rituals used in Freemasonry and those used in the Ancient Mystery Religions. The method employed by Freemasonry – the use of ritual, symbols and allegory – resonates with the Ancient Mysteries. Although it would be wrong to imply that a direct connection between the Ancient Mysteries and Freemasonry exists, there is no denying that they were of interest to students of the Occult in the seventeenth and eighteenth centuries. Bremmer states in his title, *Initiation into the Mysteries of the Ancient World*:

> *In the Age of Enlightenment, which was also the age of secret societies such as the Freemasons and the Rosicrucians, the Mysteries became a popular subject and could be seen as the place where the enlightened elite was educated, where monotheism was taught or where the immortality of the soul was affirmed, to mention only some of the more imaginative treatises.*[1]

Freemasonry has been influenced from very diverse sources alongside the Hermetic and Humanist influences from the Renaissance. There is also an important imprint left on Freemasonry by the Enlightenment. In this sense, Freemasonry is inherently linked to the birth of the modern age and has played a very important part in the genesis of modern nations such as the United States but if we were to look for a practical and enduring trait of Freemasonry aside from the ritual itself – of which there are many variants – Freemasonry is also a quest for the Self. Masonic ritual provides the initiate with the framework in which this quest for the Self can be at the very least be attempted. The objective of the hermetic space within the Masonic Lodge is to create an environment of inspiration and learning for the individual in order for him to gain a deeper understanding of himself, and to express

---

[1] Bremmer Jan. N *Initiation into the Mysteries of the Ancient World*, Walter de Gruyter GmbH, Berlin/ Boston (2014*)*

the true nature that lies within. Also to develop in such a way so that one's true nature shines out whatever the circumstance.

The ideals of tolerance and respect, which are embedded in Freemasonry, allow this process to take place without the interference of dogma and prejudice.

In the words of the celebrated Masonic writer Walter Leslie Wilmshurst:

> *The very essence of the Masonic doctrine is that all men in this world are in search of something in their own nature which they have lost, but that with proper instruction and by their own patience and industry they may hope to find. Its philosophy implies that this temporal world is the antipodes of another and more real world from which we originally came and to which we may accelerate our return by such a course of self-knowledge and self-discipline as our teaching inculcates.*[2]

In regard to what Freemasonry attempts to do, I feel compelled to include a further definition not of Freemasonry itself but of its raison d'être from Masonic historian and Jesuit Priest, José Antonio Ferrer Benimeli:

> *...But man, also needs to know where he comes from, which is the finality of his life on earth and what will happen after death. This is why when an organization affords him the chance to penetrate into the mysteries of life and death aside from religion, frequently man will easily become involved in such an organization.*[3]

For some Freemasons, the implication of the existence of a life after death will be anathema and for their benefit I will also include

---

[2] Wilmshurst W.L, *The Meaning of Masonry,* Chapter I pages 35-36 P.Lund, Humphris & Co; W.Rider & Son, London 1922.
[3] Ferrer Benimeli, J A *Masoneria, Iglesia, Revolucion e Independencia* Editorial Pontificia universidad Javeriana, (Bogota -Colombia January 2015).

the following quote from another famous Masonic author, Daniel Béresniak:

> 'The mason's viewpoint can be defined by two ideas which are repeated again and again during all Masonic rites: 'To reach further' and 'To gather what is scattered'. It is by responding to these exhortations that progress is made towards objective knowledge. For the mental processes which are needed to develop these theories and their practical applications involve acts of synthesis, association and application. It is these things which are vital for the completion of the mason's project".[4]

**What makes Freemasonry distinct from other pursuits?**

It is the use of ritual and symbolism within Freemasonry that makes it distinct from other pursuits.

**What is the purpose and use of ritual and symbolism used in Freemasonry?**

The dictionary defines ritual as: 'A religious or solemn ceremony involving a series of actions performed according to a set order.' We could argue that ritual is an expression of our inner lives, of our subconscious, unlike mundane rituals such as combing our hair, drinking coffee, or reading the newspaper. Masonic ritual works as a psychodrama, involving the use of drama, role play and theatrical elements, to stage, as it were, its legends and allegorical teachings. Psychodramas help us accept and understand our condition as humans and to look inside ourselves. The legends and teachings imparted through Masonic ritual perpetuate our ideas of birth, death and resurrection as well as our hopes and aspirations; these legends give us a narrative and a meaning. But this is a meaning unburdened by dogma that lends itself to multiple interpretations. On a more basic level, Masonic ritual could simply be considered a pedagogical method: by use of repetition the

---

[4]Béresniak,, D *Symbols of Freemasonry*, Assouline Publishing NY, 2000

lessons contained in the ritual books of Freemasonry are learned and reinforced.

The fact that Freemasonry is 'veiled in allegory and illustrated by symbols' tells us that it cannot be fully approached in a discursive, intellectual way. Freemasonry must be experienced through ritual. During the course of Masonic initiation, the candidate is totally removed from his mundane surroundings and partakes in a spiritual quest or journey of self-discovery. The Masonic analogy between building a temple and building the Self is a powerful one. Freemasonry 'builds this Temple of the Self' precisely through ritual, through the repetition of those 'words and actions arranged by a set order.' By affirming the words of the ritual over and over again, the participants are highlighting their desire for meaning and implanting these ideals and morals in their subconscious and, ultimately, giving them form and expression in reality.

If we know who we are we may know better what we want – what is really worth wanting in an increasingly materialistic world devoid of meaning. How can we hope to understand the needs of others if we do not know our own needs first?

Because of the operative past of Freemasonry, most Masonic symbols are derived from the building trade. In this sense, the famous Masonic symbols of the Compasses and the Square have a different meaning in a Masonic context. Among other possible interpretations, in Masonic ritual the Compasses usually symbolise the spiritual realm and the Square firmness and moral rectitude. Other symbols in Freemasonry are universal, such as the Sun and the Moon and yet others derive from specific cultural contexts, such as the *hexalpha* or the all-seeing eye. The all-seeing eye is a Christian symbol representing God and Providence but it can also be related to the Eye of Horus in Egyptian symbolism and in Freemasonry it represents God or the Transcendence. The question that always comes up when the topic of Masonic symbolism is discussed, why is it necessary to use symbols? One reason is that symbols allow individuals a variety of possible interpretations. It is important to remember that Freemasonry is all about interpretation and free thought. There must be a limit to this array of possible interpretations, but even so symbols by their very nature, allow Freemasons to constantly re-think the possible meanings of Masonic ritual and symbolism and apply these realisations to their own life. The by-product of this process is freedom of thought and creativity and when combined with the unusual setting of the Masonic lodge and the archaic language of the rituals it allows the participants to detach themselves from their day-to-day lives and provide them with a space where members can explore, discuss and contemplate upon subjects pertaining to deeper matters.

We cannot really speak of Freemasonry in the singular but rather of *Freemasonries* in the plural because although some Masonic Orders believe themselves to be the sole exponents of Freemasonry, there are many different Masonic Orders in the world and each has a different emphasis on the Masonic work carried out in their lodges. For some, Freemasonry is all about form, protocol and charitable works. For others the focus is placed on the spiritual and intellectual dimension of the rituals and symbols and there are others for whom Freemasonry's prime objectives are socio-political. The easiest and less opaque way of discussing these different types of Freemasonry is by splitting Freemasonry into its two main branches:

### 1. Anglo-Saxon Freemasonry

Also known as Regular or Dogmatic Freemasonry it originated in the British Isles. Regular, Anglo-Saxon Freemasonry has its emphasis on the 1717 landmarks which forbid the admission of women and atheists. In addition to this, regular Masonic Orders only recognise one Masonic jurisdiction per region or territory. The United Grand Lodge of England and all the Masonic Grand Lodges in amity with it throughout the world are the main representatives of the regular branch of Freemasonry.

### 2. Liberal or Continental Freemasonry

Also known as French or Continental Freemasonry allows with some exceptions the admission of women and atheists. Liberal Freemasonry does not have any issue with the fact that there can be more than one Masonic Order in any given territory or jurisdiction. Orders like Le Grand Orient de France and Le Droit Humain, among many others such as the Gran Loggia D'Italia, the George Washington Union or the Gran Logia Simbólica Española are exponents of the Liberal branch of Freemasonry.

*Hiram Abiff the architect of King Solomon's Temple - Sergio Simancas*

# CHAPTER 2: The Origins

### Where did Freemasonry come from?

There are many different theories of origin, but one might say that the operative theory is the most satisfactory one. The reason being is that the foundation of Masonic symbolism is taken from the building trade; this adds a substantial weight to this theory, although there are Masonic authors who oppose it.

I would not suggest that Freemasonry as we know it today owes its whole existence to operative Freemasonry and the medieval guilds. Freemasonry is a sea into which many rivers flow: Renaissance ideas, Humanism, Alchemy, the Western mystery tradition, the philosophies of the Enlightenment and the Revolutions of the eighteenth and nineteenth centuries, are all subsequent strands which were built upon the foundation of the medieval guilds of builders, including their rituals and symbolism.

### The Operatives

The medieval guilds of builders had their own rituals of admission for new members and these rituals gave a sacramental veneer to their work, thus elevating and bestowing upon the trade and its workers a sense of worth and dignity. This in turn, added a spiritual and mystical dimension to their work in daily life. The use of rituals was a common practice used in other trades from pork butchers to haberdashers.

The guilds of operative builders in the Middle Ages were well organised. The nature of their work meant that they travelled extensively, in a time in which society was extremely stratified – most people lived and died in the same town or village where they had been born without ever setting foot elsewhere. The work of these operative masons also kept them in close contact with the Church and Monastic Orders such as the Cistercians. Regardless of how Freemasonry has progressed since its inception, there is no denying that Freemasonry even to this date owes its existence to Christian mysticism and spirituality. The spiritual aspect of these operative rituals or charges came via the only religion in Europe at the time and that was of course Christianity. This introduction of Christian spirituality into the workplace is a very particular feature of Operative Freemasonry.

*Medieval Operative Freemasonry as seen by artist Sergio Simancas*

A plausible theory that explains the 'secret' words and tokens (or handshakes) of Freemasonry posits that the origin of these words and tokens can be found in the medieval guilds of operative builders whereby builders looking for work would be able to prove their credentials as reputable builders by use of these words and tokens, due to the fact that paper was not a readily accessible commodity and documents could be easily forged. The strength of the 'operative' theory rests amongst other things on the rituals of admission and articles employed by these guilds of medieval builders, the so-called 'Ancient Charges.'

**The Ancient Charges**

One of the earliest documents of this type is the *Halliwell Manuscript*, also known as the *Regius Poem* written between 1390 and 1425. The objective of this manuscript is twofold: on one hand to provide a set of rules and regulations related to the building trade, this is to say a formative goal, and on the other through the use of legend and myth to imbue the members of the trade with a sense of uniqueness and even of elitism, providing it with its own narrative and history within the framework of the prevalent Catholicism of the day.

What is most interesting about the legend told in the *Regius Manuscript* in relation to Freemasonry is the fact that it discusses Geometry making direct allusion to Euclid as well as to Ancient Egypt, all three topics present in some form or other in contemporary Masonic ritual and practice. King Athelstan is also mentioned in the manuscript and I note this because one such named side order exists in Freemasonry today, namely the Masonic Order of Athelstan. Prayers open and close the Manuscript, giving these charges a spiritual dimension.

The *Matthew Cooke Manuscript* dated somewhere around 1450 has arguably more proto-Masonic elements in it, for example a section on the Seven Liberal Arts and Sciences, prominent in the second degree of Freemasonry,

> *How, and in what manner this worthy Science of Geometry took its rise, I will tell you, as I said before. You must know that there are seven Liberal sciences, from which seven all other sciences and crafts in the world sprung; but especially is Geometry the first cause of all the other sciences, whatsoever they be. These seven sciences are as follows: The first, which is called the foundation of all science, is grammar, which teaches to write and speak correctly. The second is rhetoric, which teaches us to speak elegantly. The third is dialectic, which teaches us to discern the true from the false, and it is usually called art or sophistry [logic]. The fourth is arithmetic, which instructs us in the science of numbers, to reckon, and to make accounts. The fifth is Geometry, which teaches us all about mensuration, measures and weights, of all kinds of handicrafts. The sixth is music, and that teaches the art of singing by notation for the voice, on the organ, trumpet, and harp, and of all things pertaining thereto. The seventh is astronomy, which*

*teaches us the course of the sun and of the moon and of the other stars and planets of heaven.* "[5]

There is also an insistence on Geometry being 'chief' among the remaining arts and sciences. Further allusions to Egypt and also to Pythagoras and the Temple of Solomon are very relevant to modern Freemasonry. The document attempts to provide a direct linear narrative connecting Masonic knowledge from the Old Testament with Ancient Egypt and then via Solomon's Temple with France and England again through King Athelstan. Some of the 'secret' words of Freemasonry appear in this manuscript and are employed in Masonic ritual today.

Masonic writer and editor of the respected Spanish magazine *Cultura Masónica,* Ignacio Méndez-Trelles elaborates the importance of the Cooke Manuscript as follows:

*The Cooke Manuscript is very important from the viewpoint of the connection existing between these types of documents and the fact that Anderson himself used it to compile his Constitutions (in particular the section occupying lines 901 to 960). It seems a matter of fact that George Payne was also in possession of this document during the time he was the Grand Master of the Grand Lodge of England in 1720 and adopted it as the internal regulations of the order.* "[6]

---

5 Méndez Trelles, I Textos fundamentales de la Masoneria, Masonica Es. Asturias 2009

6 .https://archive.org/stream/The_Cooke_Manuscript_1450/The_Cooke_Manuscript_1450_djvu.txt

*Saint John, one of the original patron Saints of Freemasonry by M. Martinez Brunete*

James Anderson (1680-1739) was a Presbyterian clergyman who wrote the famous Constitutions of 1723 which are upheld today by Masonic orders, such as the United Grand Lodge of England, as the basis for Masonic regularity worldwide. The United Grand Lodge of England is one of the most respected Masonic Orders in the world so it is important not to underestimate the importance of these early Masonic documents in shaping modern day Freemasonry.

But speculative Freemasons do not build cathedrals or any other buildings, at least not in any literal sense. The analogy often used is that modern day Freemasons 'build the Temple within.' The key is in the word 'speculative'. But how did this transition occur?

# The Transition from Operative Freemasonry to Speculative Freemasonry

The Reformation (1517-1648) enforced by Henry VIII and the Dissolution of the Monasteries, resulted in a huge impact not only on religious life but it also resulted in the decline in the number of operative masons at work and attending lodges.

Operative lodges and their Ancient Charges, rites of admission and regulations were perhaps the foundation of what came to be known as speculative Freemasonry. These lodges were composed of men who were not associated with the building trade and also used the old operative rituals and charges for different purposes. Amongst the learned it was fashionable to join one of these operative lodges.

One of the first recorded initiation rituals of a non-operative Freemason was the initiation of Elias Ashmole (1617-1692). Ashmole is a fascinating character. He was a solicitor, a Royalist soldier during the English Civil war and a man with many different interests, ranging from esoteric studies such as the Cabbala and Rosicrucianism to the emerging sciences and philosophies of the Renaissance. He was initiated in a lodge in Warrington in 1646 alongside his brother-in-law, Colonel Henry Mainwaring who was fighting on the Parliamentarian side. It is possible to speculate that the prohibition of the discussion of political and religious matters in open lodge stems from this period in which religion and politics were divisive forces and maybe, in a small way, Freemasonry acted as an antidote to this division and strife. Mainwaring and other associates, many of them Freemasons, went on to create the Royal Society and thereby laid down the foundations for modern science; Isaac Newton although not a Freemason was attuned to all these Masonic ideas and wrote extensively on subjects such as alchemy and biblical interpretation.

Here we can see a new and enduring strand in Freemasonry: on the one hand many were involved in the creation of the Royal Society and in science but yet, at the same time, threads of Western esotericism were also sewn into Freemasonry. Without this seeming paradox, science and philosophy were able to sit side by side with alchemical, Cabbalistic and Hermetic pursuits. This flexibility extends to all different branches and rituals within Freemasonry, it has become one of its greatest strengths. It is precisely this flexibility, tolerance and openness to interpret Freemasonry and its symbols which make Freemasonry still relevant today.

The transition from Operative Freemasonry to Speculative Freemasonry was a slow and gradual one, as Cooper explains in his book, *Cracking the Freemason's Code*. At the time, in the late seventeenth and early eighteenth centuries there were traditional stonemason lodges, for example, Kilwinning in Scotland as well as mixed membership lodges in Aberdeen. These lodges included both operative and speculative members (it is in this sense that the word 'mixed' is used in this particular example). In addition to this there were also lodges which had no operative members at all, such as the lodge in Haughfoot in 1702.

In his book *The Genesis of Freemasonry*, David Harrison makes reference to Margaret Jacob's work *Living the Enlightenment*, which provides a very good explanation as to how this transition came about in practical terms:

> *In her work Living the Enlightenment, Margaret Jacob argues that in the late 17th century, local craft guild systems were being replaced by Masonic lodges. The old operative Masonic guilds of the medieval period transformed into a more speculative ceremonial society, developing a firm mathematical and geometrical basis (rather than the more mythical substance of its roots) and keeping an element of political control. The process saw non–masons enter Masonic guilds; the gentlemen that entered were of the gentry and merchant class, and were granted the privileges and freedom of the town. Jacobs looks at an operative mason's guild in Dundee as an example which in the 1690s was in decline with low membership and in need of new blood; the area itself suffering from reduced population and economic problems. A document dated November 1700, stated that the guild should give strangers the benefit of their freedom for the price of 10 pounds, a new proposal that*

*they hoped would help aid the economic problems of the guild.*[7]

One can only speculate what may have attracted people such as Elias Ashmole to these transitioning operative lodges. Ashmole was a Rosicrucian and was very interested in the esoteric arts, what we would now perhaps call the Occult. It would seem that the Ancient Charges, the rituals and ceremonies used by these operative lodges were a great part of the attraction. The fact that these lodge meetings provided men from different backgrounds, political ideas and religious denominations a safe, shared space may also have lured cultivated men from the Renaissance who had experienced the horrors of the English Civil war.

The association between the army and Freemasonry is a very old one and as Alberto Moreno explains in great detail in his blog *Masoneria Antigua*, one of the earliest records of a purely speculative non-operative Masonic lodge is the consecration of Youghal Lodge in Ireland in 1695. The membership of the lodge was made up almost exclusively of British soldiers stationed in the Irish port of the same name and the lodge worked continuously until 1830 when it finally surrendered its warrant, although as Alberto Moreno states there is currently a Masonic lodge working in Youghal today.

### The United Grand Lodge of England

Members from four London speculative lodges formed a Grand Lodge in 1717, after meeting at the Goose and Gridiron public house in London. The first Grand Master was Anthony Sayer. In 1721, clergyman James Anderson, who held high Masonic office, was commissioned to write a revised version of the Old Charges which was published in 1723 as the *Constitutions of the Freemasons*. This is a very important document which up to the present day sets out the requirements for regularity and recognition by the United Grand Lodge of England. Any Masonic organisation

---

[7] Harrison, D *The Genesis of Freemasonry*, Lewis Masonic, UK 2014.

that does not comply with these landmarks simply does not exist as such, in the eyes of the United Grand Lodge of England.

The Constitutions set out the landmarks for so-called Masonic regularity: only men can be admitted into Freemasonry, belief in a Supreme Being is compulsory and there can only be one Masonic jurisdiction in any given country.

These landmarks were revised by officials of the United Grand Lodge of England in 1929 and are followed today by all Grand Lodges in amity with the United Grand Lodge of England:

### Basic Principles for Grand Lodge Recognition

(Accepted by Grand Lodge, 4 September 1929 The M.W. Grand Master)

> The Grand Master having expressed a desire that the Board would draw up a statement of the basic principles on which this Grand Lodge could be invited to recognise any Grand Lodge applying for recognition by the English Jurisdiction, the Board of General Purposes has gladly complied. The result, as follows, has been approved by the Grand Master, and it will form the basis of a questionnaire to be forwarded in future to each Jurisdiction requesting English recognition. The Board desires that not only such bodies but the Brethren generally throughout the Grand Master's Jurisdiction shall be fully informed as to those Basic Principles of Freemasonry for which the Grand Lodge of England has stood throughout its history.
>
> 1. Regularity of origin; i.e. each Grand Lodge shall have been established lawfully by a duly recognised Grand Lodge or by three or more regularly constituted Lodges.
> 2. That a belief in the G.A.O.T.U. (The Great Architect of the Universe) and His revealed will shall be an essential qualification for membership.
> 3. That all Initiates shall take their Obligation on or in full view of the open Volume of the Sacred Law, by which is meant the revelation from above which is

binding on the conscience of the particular individual who is being initiated.
4. That the membership of the Grand Lodge and individual Lodges shall be composed exclusively of men; and that each Grand Lodge shall have no Masonic intercourse of any kind with mixed Lodges or bodies which admit women to membership.
5. That the Grand Lodge shall have sovereign jurisdiction over the Lodges under its control; that it shall be a responsible, independent, self-governing organisation, with sole and undisputed authority over the Craft or Symbolic Degrees (Entered Apprentice, Fellow Craft, and Master Mason) within its Jurisdiction; and shall not in any way be subject to, or divide such authority with, a Supreme Council or other Power claiming any control or supervision over those degrees.
6. That the three Great Lights of Freemasonry (namely, the Volume of the Sacred Law, the Square, and the Compasses) shall always be exhibited when the Grand Lodge or its subordinate Lodges are at work, the chief of these being the Volume of the Sacred Law.
7. That the discussion of religion and politics within the Lodge shall be strictly prohibited.
8. That the principles of the Antient Landmarks, customs, and usages of the Craft shall be strictly observed.[8]

A Lodge or Grand Lodge, if it wishes to be considered 'regular,' cannot accept women or atheists as members. It also may not have any Masonic connection to a lodge or Masonic Order that does. It is of course the prerogative of the United Grand Lodge of England to choose who can or cannot join their organisation and given some of the scandals and abuses which have occurred in the past it is easy to understand why the United Grand Lodge of England holds on to its foundational documents and traditions so

---

8 Information for the guidance of members of the Craft, United Grand Lodge of England 2014 (online resource http://www.ugle.org.uk/about/book-of-constitutions)

fiercely. But overall, this judgement has been detrimental to Freemasonry and created a divided and divisive fraternity.

Let us return to the eighteenth century. In 1725 the Grand Lodge of Ireland was established and in 1736 the Scottish followed suit and created their Grand Lodge of Scotland, although there is evidence of speculative lodges in Scotland and Ireland that precede speculative lodges in England.

Freemasonry spread throughout Europe and beyond, with the first North American Grand Lodge being founded in 1731. In 1751 members of six London lodges with a large Irish membership created what is now known as the *Grand Lodge of the Antients*. Under the leadership of Laurence Dermott, the famous Masonic book of constitutions *Ahiman Rezon* or *Help to a Brother,* was published as an alternative to Anderson's Constitutions. The *Grand Lodge of the Antients* rivalled the original Premier Grand Lodge of England of 1717, mostly on the basis that the latter had made too many changes in the ritual and established customs. After 63 years both Grand lodges merged to form the United Grand Lodge of England which is to date the most prestigious Masonic Order in existence and the self-appointed guardian of Masonic regularity. Although, Freemasonry was not always split the development of Freemasonry in the European continent was different and followed its own distinct path, particularly in France.

*The United Grand Lodge of England in London as seen by Mayu Omori*

# CHAPTER 3: French Freemasonry

## Some Early Fringe Orders

Liberal Freemasonry as we know it was born in the nineteenth century. This was a result of Le Grand Orient de France rescinding the requirement that an aspirant wishing to join Freemasonry had to declare a belief in a Supreme Being. This action resulted in the United Grand Lodge of England withdrawing their recognition of Le Grand Orient de France. Moreover, this event was really a reflection of the differences between, French and English Freemasonry which had developed over nearly two centuries

Are there any early examples of Masonic Orders or Lodges deviating from regular landmarks? Are there any precedents for what we call today Liberal Freemasonry? There are anecdotal instances such as the initiation of Elizabeth Aldworth, an Irish woman who in 1710 accidentally caught her father and his Masonic brethren in the middle of a lodge meeting and was subsequently initiated in order to avoid any Masonic secrets being in possession of outsiders to Freemasonry. In 1778, Hannah Mather Crocker and other women founded an all-female lodge in Boston in the USA.

The Rite of Strict Observance is an early example of what many regular Freemasons would have most certainly deemed to be fringe or irregular Freemasonry. The degrees of this Rite were created in the late eighteenth century and conferred by the Order of Strict Observance. The Rite was mainly a German creation introduced initially by Baron Karl Gotthelf von Hund. The Rite's main purpose was rather contradictory. On the one hand the main objective was to return to a 'purer' form of Freemasonry, paying close attention to form and discipline and shunning the more mainstream occultist practices which were so widespread in Freemasonry at the time, whilst on the other hand professing a belief in the guidance of the *Superiores Incogniti* or Unknown Superiors. The Order of Strict Observance had also another objective, to restore the Order of the Knights Templar. The existence of a mysterious group of almost superhuman beings in possession of esoteric truths secretly directing the destiny of humanity is a concept which may have started with the Rosicrucian manifestos of the sixteenth century and which has since been a constant in the occultist tradition from Madame Blavatsky and the Theosophists through to Aleister Crowley.

*The enigmatic Count Cagliostro by Sergio Simancas*

It was in one of the lodges of this Order of Strict Observance working in London where Giuseppe Balsamo – also known as Count Cagliostro – was allegedly initiated. Cagliostro, born in Italy in 1743, claimed to have travelled to Mecca as a young man with his master, the alchemist Althotas. He then supposedly travelled to Egypt where he studied the Hermetic arts. Cagliostro also travelled to Malta where he was, according to his own words, admitted into the Order of Malta where he discovered the secrets of the Jewish Cabbala and Magic. These were all subjects of great interest in the eighteenth century, a period in which humanist philosophy was challenging the foundations of established religion. As a reaction to the rationalist zeal of humanist philosophy new forms of arcane knowledge and spirituality were being sought. The discovery of the *Corpus Hermeticum* in the 1400s had started this interest in the Egyptian mysteries.

Cagliostro was initiated in 1776 into a Strict Observance Lodge in London's Soho with his wife. He supposedly found a booklet written by an occultist called George Coston in a London bookshop which contained the sources of the Egyptian ritual he would go on to write. In their book *The Masonic Magician*, Faulks and Cooper state that the famous Victorian Freemason and occultist John Yarker (1833-1913) believed the real source for Cagliostro's Egyptian Rite to be Martinez Pasqually's Masonic rite which included magic and theurgy. Whatever may have been the case, Cagliostro's Egyptian Rite of Freemasonry or Rite of Misraim combined Masonic ritual with theurgy, Hermetic philosophy and other esoteric elements. The order itself was established in 1779. The Rite consisted of the working of degrees from the 4th to the 9th and continues to exist to this date although in 1838, Jacques Etienne Marconis de Nègre (1795-1865) created the Rite of Memphis as a variant of the original Rite created by Cagliostro and which focused more on Templarism. In 1881 the Italian General Garibaldi (1807-1882) merged the old Rite of Misraim with the Memphis Rite created by Marconis de Negre.

Today there is a website for the Ancient and Primitive Rite of Memphis-Misraim in the United Kingdom with links to branches in other parts of the world as well as other orders styling themselves as Misraim or Egyptian Freemasonry.

These Masonic rites did not conform to the norm and sought alternative ways of understanding Freemasonry and in this sense, I would consider them to be worthy of inclusion in a book on Liberal and Adogmatic Freemasonry.

### French or Continental Freemasonry

Freemasonry in France developed in a very different way and I believe this is due essentially to the fact that whilst in England the medieval and operative roots of Freemasonry weighed more heavily, by the time speculative Freemasonry reached France the zeitgeist under which it developed was a very different one. French

Freemasonry inherited the mystical influences from its English counterpart; however, the influence of the Enlightenment in the genesis of French Freemasonry cannot be underestimated.

Freemasonry was brought to France by English Jacobites in the 1680s. It is said that the first lodge in France was consecrated in 1728. Thanks partly to the admiration for British societies and institutions in continental Europe at the time, Freemasonry became fashionable in France. Initially, Freemasonry was viewed with suspicion by the French authorities, but by 1737 there were many French members in these British lodges. In 1738 the first French Grand Master, the Duc d' Antin, was elected and between the years 1771-73, Le Grande Loge de France, later known as Le Grand Orient de France, was created.

In England Freemasonry quickly became part of the establishment but in France it was to follow a different path. Initially Freemasonry in France attracted the aristocracy and also, in cities such as Lyon, the bourgeoisie. The famous 1737 discourse of the Chevalier de Ramsay (1686-1743) played an important part in the genesis of French Freemasonry. Ramsay was a Jacobite who relocated to France in 1724. He was also a *quietist*, a follower of Spanish Mystic Miguel de Molinos. *Quietism* was a form of Christianity which focused on contemplation and silence above other more traditional forms of religious practice. It is interesting to note since it is an example of the new forms of spirituality which were emerging during this period.

In his famous *Discourse Pronounced at the Reception of Freemasons by Monsieur Ramsay,* the Chevalier provided some defining criteria for what a Freemason should be and what was the purpose of the institution itself. For Ramsay, a Freemason was a man who was defined by having a charitable disposition and an appreciation for art and culture as well as a capacity for exercising discretion at all times.

Ramsay did two more things in his *Discourse*: he provided Freemasonry with a genealogical origin by linking it to the Order of the Knights Templar and the Crusades thereby introducing a new set of chivalric symbolism in the process. He also described the international and progressive traits that many modern Masonic liberal and orders uphold and live by to this day:

> *Mankind is not essentially distinguished by the tongues spoken, the clothes worn, the lands occupied or the dignities with which it is invested. The world is nothing but a huge republic, of which every nation is a family, every individual a child. Our Society was at the outset established to revive and spread these essential maxims borrowed from the nature of man.*[9]

French Freemasonry developed in the eighteenth century and the influence of the Enlightenment cannot be emphasised enough. We must not forget the addition of chivalric and Templar symbolism added to Masonic ritual in France. Nor can we ignore the esoteric strands still carried by the influence of the Renaissance. This would result later in a Freemasonry which employed a mystical and deeply esoteric ritual but which had, as a whole, a philosophical and humanist outlook occasionally verging on the socio-political.

So how did all this come about?

## Philosophical and Literary Influences

The Enlightenment brought all old ideas and dogmas into question and was the logical consequence of the Renaissance when gradually the medieval God-centred view of the world gave way to man as the study of man. No motto sums up better the Enlightenment than Kant's often quoted 'Dare to know! Have the courage to use your own reason'. The American and French Revolutions were direct consequences of the new ways of thinking inspired by the Enlightenment. Science, law, religion, philosophy and politics were radically changed by the ideas of this period and the old regime gradually gave way to the Industrial Revolution and the birth of modernity. Isaac Newton invented modern science, Diderot and his Encyclopaedia showed the world a new source of knowledge independent from religion and the whole structure on which society had been based on up to that moment was challenged and turned upside down.

---

[9] http://ecossais.net/html/ramsay-s_oration.html

*Marianne: prevailing symbol of the French Republic by M. Martinez Brunete*

A new way of understanding the world through the use of rational discourse was changing society. Freemasonry spread through the emergence of coffee shops and literary salons. Many saw Freemasonry at the time as a 'formative school for men.' Plato's Republic could perhaps be considered one of the first attempts at describing what a perfect society should look like and it is no surprise that Classical Greco-Roman philosophy became an important influence in this period. The Renaissance that preceded the Enlightenment was a period in which, after centuries of scholasticism, man finally turned his attention to the Classical period again.

In Sir Francis Bacon's utopian novel, *The New Atlantis* (published circa 1624) Bacon relates how a group of Europeans are stranded in a fictitious South American island inhabited by an evolved society which has its own version of the Royal Society, the so-called House of Solomon, a topic which of course would have resonated with any Freemason reading the book in the eighteenth century. The influence of works such as *Utopia* by Sir Thomas More and *The City of the Sun* by Tommaso Campanella as well as satires such as Rabelais' *Gargantua and Pantagruel* were influential in the seventeenth and eighteenth centuries alongside contemporary works of the time such as *Gulliver's Travels* by Swift, *Code de la Nature* by E. G. Morelly and *Candide* by Voltaire. There was a hunger for creating a new world, for breaking down social barriers, challenging old dogmas and power bases, abolishing slavery, giving equality to women and creating the 'perfect' society. It seems apt, as the eighteenth century drew to a close, for Kant to have written his *Perpetual Peace: A Philosophical sketch* in which he boldly defines ideals that are still relevant today in the twenty-first century.

*An impression of The Age of Enlightenment by Sergio Simancas*

But let us hear some of these and figures from the Enlightenment in their own words:

*Upon the progress of knowledge, the whole progress of the human race is immediately dependent: he, who retards that, hinders this also.*

Johann Gottlieb Fichte, initiated in 1749


*One ought, every day at least, to hear a little song, read a good poem, see a fine picture, and, if it were possible, to speak a few reasonable words.*

Johann Wolfgang von Goethe, initiated in 1780

*Think wrongly if you wish to, but in all instances, think by yourself.*

Gotthold Ephraim Lessing, initiated in 1771.

*I disapprove of what you say but I will defend to the death your right to say it.*

Voltaire, initiated in 1778

*Freemasonry is a community of men...who reflect on the progress of humanity and work in silence.*

Johann Gottfried Herder, initiated in 1776.


In the context of Freemasonry, and I personally understand Freemasonry as a spiritual and intellectual path of self-improvement, I think it is essential to focus not only on the social changes brought about by the Age of Enlightenment but also by the new ways of understanding spirituality outside the confines of the Church which made their appearance during this period. Voltaire, himself a Freemason – albeit that he was initiated during the last year of his life – promoted one of these new ways of understanding spirituality, namely Deism. Freemasonry has always been accused by the Church of being Deist and it's partly on the back of this accusation that some Papal Bull's against Freemasonry have been issued.

Deism is a belief in God, or a Supreme Being, Arche or Prima Causa that disregards dogma and organised religion and views the deities of all religions as being interpretations of the same Truth or Higher Power.

Deism also promotes the idea of a God or Higher Power who does not necessarily intervene in human affairs. In a way this solves one of the biggest theological dilemmas for any inquisitive mind, that is the problem of the existence of evil in the world.

François-Marie Arouet known as Voltaire was born in 1694 in Paris and initiated into Freemasonry in 1778. He was a writer, a philosopher and a vociferous critic of the Church. Like many of his contemporaries he was fascinated by the British political system and lived in London in 1728. He was admired by the French Revolutionaries who were inspired by his work. Voltaire expressed a tolerance for members of other races and religions, a stance which is admirable for a European man of the eighteenth century. He was a complex character and believed the Bible and Christianity to be absurdities.

Atheism was also put forward in no uncertain terms during the Age of Enlightenment. One only needs to talk to a convinced Atheist today to realise that Atheism is another religion and to an extent another way of understanding spirituality by annihilating it perhaps but an alternative way of dealing with the subject nonetheless. Atheism had been espoused in the previous century by Spinoza and Pierre Bayle and a very good example of an eighteenth-century atheist is the figure of the Baron d'Holbach who hosted an exclusive literary salon in Paris frequented by Benjamin Franklin, Rousseau, Diderot, David Hume and Horace Walpole among many other distinguished guests. Baron d'Holbach contributed to the Encyclopaedia and wrote a series of essays that laid the foundations of Philosophical Materialism which influenced the writings of Karl Marx. There does not seem to be any evidence that d'Holbach was a Freemason, however he definitely embodied the most radical version of the spirit of his age.

The Age of Enlightenment gave birth to the modern age and although we now live in the murky, anxiety-ridden postmodern age and can look back at the twentieth century critically and see many of its bad points, there is no doubt that in spite of the horrors of two World Wars and the atomic bomb, modernity has increased living standards and life expectancy at least in the developed world. The Age of Enlightenment was the age when concepts such as freedom of conscience, equality and secularism or laïcité were starting to be sketched leading to the socialism of the nineteenth century.

It is easy to see how a Freemason with a penchant for historical analysis may look back at the Enlightenment period in awe and hold on to the notion that this period was one of Masonic splendour and although not all the key figures of the Enlightenment were, many active revolutionaries certainly were.

In a sense it is indeed tempting to see this period as the golden age of Freemasonry and perhaps this was the case. But then, how can Freemasonry be relevant today if it looks back so far for validation? Masonic writer Javier Otaola provides us with an answer in his superb article *La Ilustración Escarmentada* (The Chastened Enlightenment),

> *The Enlightenment can be defined not only as a period in human history but also as an activity, a task and not as something finished or complete...Enlightenment is also action. Act: Aufklärung,, Enlightenment...The Enlightenment starts from that viewpoint, the Sapere Aude of Kant, the will to not be subdued and to never give up the right to reason and the risks that are implicit to it. Once we have made that jump and assumed these risks the Enlightenment is open ended, an ongoing process; it's no coincidence that both the Enlightenment and the birth of speculative Freemasonry took place in the eighteenth century.*[10]

To consider that the Enlightenment is still an ongoing project that has not yet fully achieved its full potential is perhaps the best way to justify the existence and the purpose of Freemasonry today. However, this argument will be less persuasive for many who see

---

[10] Otaola, J La Ilustración Escarmentada, Cultura Masonica edition 25 Masonica Es Spain 2016

Freemasonry and its place in the world in a different way. English Freemasonry owes more to the Renaissance than to the Enlightenment and this might be why English regular Freemasonry has remained more inert, less progressive and attached to its landmarks.

### Mystical and Chivalric Influences

In France Freemasonry was mainly influenced by the Enlightenment but in its origins, as I have briefly discussed at the beginning of this chapter, it was influenced by the traditional Templar observance which in turn introduced chivalric symbolism.

In their excellent book *Freemasonry: A French View*, Dachez and Bauer explain that when the Count of Clermont was elected Grand Master in France in 1743, he stated that only "gentlemen and good bourgeois men" were eligible as members. Many Worshipful Masters remained in their positions for life during this period and Freemasonry was initially more elitist in France than it was in England. During the second part of the eighteenth century and prior to the French Revolution figures such as Martinez de Pasqually (1727-1774) and Cagliostro influenced Freemasonry with their own Rites and degrees, adding an esoteric dimension with links to Alchemy, Rosicrucianism and the Cabbala. So there seem to be two strands developing in Freemasonry, an esoteric and hermetic strand alongside a humanist and rationalist one. These elements can be seen in the bombastic titles of the degrees of the ritual system of choice employed in France, the Ancient and Accepted Scottish Rite.

Jean Baptiste Willermoz born in Lyon in 1710 was educated in a Jesuit school and belonged to a bourgeois family. He was the Worshipful Master of his lodge at the age of twenty and had some very interesting connections, from Martinez Pasqually to Louis Claude de Saint Martin and Baron von Hund. Willermoz represents an esoteric and alchemical strand of Freemasonry which was focused on the Great Work of the alchemists and occultists of the period. Willermoz is credited with creating the Rectified Scottish Rite, a Masonic rite which places great emphasis on Freemasonry as a system of initiation, as an initiatory society framed against an esoteric interpretation of Christianity.

For Willermoz initiation can be explained and formulated and also has a distinct metaphysical objective. It goes beyond shaking us up and making us see in a different light, it points us towards a very particular body of thought. The Rectified Scottish Rite is a Christian form of Freemasonry. Furthermore, it is a Trinitarian form of Freemasonry and it is this strand of French or Continental Freemasonry that will lead to Martinism and other schools of esoteric Christianity. Both the Rectified Scottish Rite and Martinism exist today and it is interesting to note how this particular branch of Freemasonry originated in France during the same century in which the French Revolution took place. Wasn't the French Revolution according to popular thought the work of Freemasons fighting against the Monarchy, the Church and the old regime?

## The French Revolution

*An impression of a Masonic Initiation (XVIII Century) by Sergio Simancas*

Allegedly, the French Revolution was engineered and masterminded by Freemasons such as Mirabeau, Lafayette and Danton as well as Marat, Desmoulins and Robespierre to name just a few key figures of the Revolution. But it is important to remember that although all these men I have named were Freemasons, they entertained different ideas as to how French society should evolve in the eighteenth century and ranged from being moderates to revolutionaries. Mirabeau and Lafayette believed that the monarchy still had a role to play, whereas Danton and Robespierre, for example, wanted a Republic. There were also Freemasons such as the Count François-Henri de Virieu and the Duke Montmorency-Luxembourg among many others who openly opposed the French Revolution. It is also important to note that between 1793 and 1796, during the most turbulent years of the Revolution, Le Grand Orient de France suspended all Masonic activities.

Although there are some parallels between Freemasonry and the ideals of the French Revolution, Freemasonry advocates equality, tolerance, respect and obedience to the rule of law and because of this it cannot ever be mixed up in plots, conspiracies or revolutions.

Some readers may believe that the motto of French or continental Freemasonry still used to date; "Liberty, Equality, Fraternity" was adopted during the French Revolution, but the fact is that Freemasonry only adopted this motto after the revolution of 1848. The connection between eighteenth century French Freemasonry and the French Revolution appears to be anecdotal, punctuated with some peculiarities such as Robespierre's *Cult of the Supreme Being* with its unfortunate Masonic resonance. We have to differentiate between lodges carrying out Masonic work and lodges being misused for political reasons in which the discretion and secrecy of Freemasonry were being blatantly abused. Many Freemasons lost their lives to the guillotine during the French Revolution and others had to emigrate to save their lives, while some prospered but this had nothing to do with their Masonic membership, rather it was down to their social and political circumstances as individuals.

In the words of Masonic historian José Antonio Benimeli:

> *Freemasonry was one of the first associations that suffered the consequences of the French Revolution. All one has to do is read the lists of Freemasons from Paris- members of Le Grand Orient de France published at the end of the eighteenth century by Bihan- to see how many emigrated, were subjected to deportation or executed. Most lodges had to cease their activities and from 1791 onwards the Grande Loge de France stopped working. Le Grand Orient de France followed suit in 1793. The few lodges that continued to operate in spite of all this had to*

> become "*revolutionary clubs*" as was the case with the *Amis de la Liberté* in Paris and the *Bonne Amitié* of Marseille. [11]

The famous Lodge of the Nine Sisters had members such as Benjamin Franklin, Camille Desmoulins and Voltaire amongst its ranks and because of these famous members it has been associated with this narrative of Freemasonry and Revolution. Founded in 1776, the Lodge was consecrated to promote philosophical and educational values. The Nine Sisters lodge became part of the Institut de France promoting science, arts and humanities during 1792 when it ceased its Masonic work which was re-commenced in 1805. Yes, some members of the lodge did support the American Revolution but like many other French lodges during the French Revolution it suspended its Masonic activities.

The reason Freemasonry has been accused of being revolutionary is due to the work of Augustin Barruel, a French clergyman born in 1741, who wrote a 4,000-page book dedicated to a destructive, false and misinformed attack on Freemasonry based on his own fundamentalist views. Barruel linked the alleged anticlericalism of Freemasonry to the Knights Templar who had been accused of blasphemy and satanic practices by the Church and the King of France, resulting in the execution of their Grand Master Jacques de Molay. The so-called *Illuminati of Bavaria*, a political pressure group which had infiltrated Masonic lodges in 1784, was also a source of distrust towards Freemasonry, but again what these illuminati did was misuse Masonic membership for their own means.

In 1889, during the 100-year anniversary celebration of the French Revolution the then Grand Master of Le Grand Orient de France, Frédéric Desmons equalled Freemasonry to the French Republic. Masonic values are universal values after all, but the French Republic was the result of a very complex set of historical events in eighteenth century France, not of Freemasonry which originated a couple of centuries before in a different country. Fortunately, recent books on the subject have taken a more objective and realistic approach when studying the relationship

---

[11] José Antonio Benimeli, Masoneria, Iglesia, Revolucion e Independencia. Pontificia Universidad Javeriana, Bogota (Colombia) 2015

between Freemasonry and the French Revolution. As Benimeli points out – quoting from Pierre Chevalier's book *The Sceptre, the Staff and the Square under Louis XV and Louis XVI* – Freemasonry prior to the French Revolution was apolitical and respectful of religion, which makes perfect sense given its roots in post-civil war England. Chevalier adds that the importance of Freemasonry in France during the eighteenth century hinged on the fact that by its mere existence it promoted freedom of association under an absolutist regime which contributed greatly to the development of democracy and modernity.

The Grande Loge de France was almost eradicated during the French Revolution given the fact that many of its members were aristocrats. Le Grand Orient de France had also suffered considerable losses but managed to proclaim itself as the main Masonic Order in France after the French Revolution, a place it still holds today.

# CHAPTER 4: The Birth of Liberal Freemasonry

## Le Grand Orient de France

Estimating the birth of what we understand today as Liberal Freemasonry is at best a risky business, it is possible to speculate around the year 1877 as the year in which this particular branch of Freemasonry came into existence. The catalyst being, Frédéric Desmons a Protestant priest and Grand Master of Le Grand Orient, who seconded the vote in favour of freedom of conscience at the 1877 convention of the Order. This momentous event abolished the Masonic landmark requiring a belief in a Supreme Being from its members as well as the belief in the afterlife. This is not to say that believers in God and the immortality of the soul were barred from joining Le Grand Orient de France, but rather that atheists and agnostics were now also welcome to join the Order. This meant that the United Grand Lodge of England withdrew its recognition of Le Grand Orient de France and that a new way of understanding Freemasonry had come into being.

The background to this was the influence of the historical and social period at the time: The First International of 1864 and the Paris Commune as well as the growing tensions and divisions between the conservative Catholic population of the French countryside and the progressive, socialist sector in the industrialized cities. There were some elements inherent in French Freemasonry and its development during the Enlightenment which made it more prone to change in contrast to English Freemasonry which was already part of the establishment. There was no need for English Freemasonry to reformulate its principles, as it fulfilled a very different role in British society. In England Freemasonry was certainly prospering during the nineteenth century because of its close association with the British Empire, the Church and the Monarchy. In France, during Napoleon's mandate Freemasonry also became intertwined with the political establishment albeit in a more forceful manner, since Napoleon, fearful of any revolts, exercised an absolutist control over Freemasonry nominating Grand Masters and other important officers. Up to this point, there had been unofficial relations between the United Grand Lodge of England and its American counterparts and the Grand Orient de France.

Le Grand Orient de France dates its foundation back to 1733 when the first English lodges in France had started to organize themselves into a constitutive body calling itself at the time the *Grande Loge de France*. In 1773 the name was changed to Le Grand Orient de France when the articles of constitution of the Order were revised, although some lodges objected to this and remained united under Le Grande Loge de France. Then in 1799, after the turbulent years of the French Revolution, both Orders with their numbers severely depleted, joined forces and amalgamated under the banner of the larger Grand Orient de France. In 1894, following a disagreement over the prerequisite of belief in a Supreme Being for initiates, a number of lodges separated from Le Grand Orient de France and created Le Grande Loge de France which still exists to this day, discussed later in the chapter.

In 1761, Freemason E. Morin with authorization from Le Grande Loge de France created twenty-five new Masonic degrees which were encompassed in the Rite of Perfection. These degrees were further developed and a total of eight new degrees were added including the 33rd degree or Sovereign Inspector General. Morin created his degrees in the Antilles. In 1802 a Supreme Council to oversee these higher degrees was constituted in Charleston. The problem was that in 1789 another French Freemason, Auguste de Grasse-Tilly also with authorisation created another Supreme Council in Paris. The Supreme Council and Le Grand Orient of France struggled over control of the higher degrees of the Ancient and Accepted Scottish Rite (AASR). This ended with a division between a Supreme Council allied to Le Grand Orient de France and another, separate Supreme Council of France linked to Le Grande Loge de France which continued until the end of the nineteenth century. These two Supreme Councils created to control and administer the higher degrees of the AASR were instrumental in allowing the proliferation of new Masonic orders later on.

But it was at the end of the nineteenth century with the Third French Republic that Le Grand Orient de France became openly involved in socio-political issues in a further break from traditional regular Freemasonry. It is during this period when the requisite for belief in a Supreme Being was eradicated and when the influence of positivism and the new political emphasis of the order were felt. It is also in the nineteenth century when Le Grand Orient de France identified itself institutionally with the values of the French Republic and it was then that the triad 'Liberty, Equality, Fraternity' became a Masonic leitmotif.

*The headquarters of the Grand Orient de France in Paris by Mayu Omori*

The concept of *laïcité*, so dear to Le Grand Orient de France and French Freemasonry as a whole, was born with the 1905 French law of separation between state and church. To this day, Le Grand Orient de France has a dedicated committee to the study, development and currency of secularism in French society. The topic itself is one to which countless Masonic lectures[12] have been devoted.

Freedom of conscience as implemented in Le Grand Orient de France after the 1877 Convent was a defining moment in the history of Freemasonry as a whole. The repercussions are more to do with the fact that by advocating freedom of conscience – as in the case of laïcité – Le Grand Orient de France is allying itself directly with a

---

[12] Masonic lectures are known in English as Pieces of Architecture, Planches in French and Planchas in Spanish.

particular ideology and current of thought that can be easily translated into party politics.

Universalism is another ideal highly prized by Le Grand Orient de France; the Order has around twenty lodges operating internationally aside from the 1.100 plus lodges it has in France.

The social and political dimension of the order is yet another characteristic of Le Grand Orient de France which has helped it become the paradigm of Liberal and Adogmatic Freemasonry in the world. To mention but one example, Le Grand Orient de France recently condemned the Archbishop of Paris for his stance against same-sex marriage but the Order's involvement in social and political issues has gone much deeper.

The political involvement of Le Grand Orient de France, plays an important aspect of the Order's aims and objectives, although this has occasionally backfired, most notably during the first years of the twentieth century when it was discovered that Le Grand Orient de France was making use of its Masonic connections to spy on military figures and appoint civil servants. Although, there have been other occasions where direct political involvement has yielded good fruits, for example, in 1988 President Mitterrand commissioned the Grand Master of Le Grand Orient de France, Roger Leray to mediate between Kanaks and Caledonians in New Caledonia and the negotiations met with some success. At any rate the political dimension of Le Grand Orient de France should not have any institutional links with any political party; rather its ideals and values are universal: democracy, *laïcité*, freedom of conscience, universalism, liberty, equality and fraternity.

Many high-profile figures in all fields of human endeavour have been members of Le Grand Orient de France and the list I have compiled below is based purely on my personal choice and my objective is merely to present the reader with a varied and interesting collection of people.

Although Voltaire was initiated at the end of his life and was only a Freemason for less than a year it would be unkind not to include the king of philosophers in this brief list.

Voltaire was initiated in 1778 when he was 84 years old in the lodge The Nine Sisters in Paris. Voltaire was a Deist, and it is easy to see a connection between his Masonic membership, albeit during a limited period of time, and his philosophical ideas. However, this may not be accurate, that is to say there may not be a connection between Voltaire, the enlightened philosopher, deist and man of his time and Freemasonry. Neither are there any Masonic references in his work and correspondence, or at least no direct unequivocal references to Freemasonry. But we could look at this from another angle and perhaps see Freemasonry as being influenced by these ideals rather than the opposite.

To suggest that Voltaire was an archetypal Freemason would be incorrect, rather it is perhaps truer to say that he embodied the spirit of his era and that his masonic membership could be seen to represent an example of the influences that the Enlightenment and the social developments of the eighteenth century were having on continental Freemasonry.

Emir Abdelkader, fought the French invasion of Algeria and ended up exiled in Damascus. He was initiated in 1864 in the lodge The Pyramids working under the auspices of Le Grand Orient de France. His sons were also Freemasons.

Pastor Frédéric Desmons, was a Protestant clergyman who was initiated in 1861 and who fought for the initiation of women and the implementation of freedom of conscience in Freemasonry.

Émile Combes, a more politically radical Freemason who was initiated in 1869 and who fought vigorously against the Church and was involved in the 1905 law of separation between church and state.

Daniel Béresniak (1933-2005) is perhaps one of the most important literary Masonic references of the twentieth century and for his extensive body of work is a prime representative of Liberal Freemasonry.

He was born into a family of Russian Jewish émigrés in Paris in 1933. During the Nazi occupation of France his mother and many other members of his family were murdered and he escaped to the French countryside and learned the Catholic catechism in order to pass himself off as a Christian and escape persecution. Fortunately, his father survived the war and so did Daniel Béresniak, who joined Freemasonry in 1954, influenced by the memory of his uncle Leon who died in Auschwitz. He studied philology, Aramaic and Hebrew and could speak many languages with different levels of fluency. He was an autodidact and an avid reader with an interest in philosophy, history and psychology. In the article *My Father my Brother* Daniel Béresniak's son Ariel suggests that the tragic events his father experienced as a child drew him to a life of intellectual pursuits. Although Béresniak, was initiated in Le Grand Orient de France where he spent many years as a member, in the 1970s he resigned and formed an independent masonic Order, the OITAR (*L'Ordre Initiatique et Traditionnel de l'Art Royal*). Daniel Béresniak, wrote several books: *Rites and Symbols of Freemasonry, Tomorrow Freemasonry* and *The Game of Hermes* to cite but a few. For Béresniak, knowledge can never be static and must always be in motion in the same way as the Freemason travels symbolically in his lodge. In his own words:

> *Our Work consists in killing the old man within us, the one who believes he is always in possession of the truth and who therefore reacts instead of acting. We must create a free man, a man who knows what he believes and who learns to act truthfully.* [13]

Béresniak was an advocate of diversity and of masonic pluralism and as such an important voice within Liberal Freemasonry. As a Freemason initiated in Le Grand Orient de France in the middle of the twentieth century it might be tempting to imagine his approach to Freemasonry to be rationalistic and in line with what we have come to expect from a lot of continental Freemasonry, yet his work has a historical emphasis and shows a total admiration and respect for ritual. Béresniak's work also reflects an interest in the Western mystery tradition although from a Jungian standpoint. Jose Luis Cobos, Freemason and member of the Gran Logia Simbólica Española, who met with Daniel Béresniak in 1999, explains in his article 'La Vida, un recorrido lleno de recovecos' (*Life a path filled with Nooks)* how Daniel Béresniak, viewed Geometry as a metaphor for the hope in a coherent cosmic order. This is of particular interest, since it provides an alternative way of approaching the Masonic concept of the Great Architect of the Universe and yet, it still does not remove the spiritual dimension that is inherent and essential to Freemasonry. Béresniak is a very important reference in contemporary Masonic literature but sadly, only one or perhaps two of his books are available in English. The

---

[13]Diaz, V Life and work of Daniel Béresniak,, a great Master Mason, Cultura Masonica issue 16, Asturias

language barrier is yet another divide between regular Anglo-Saxon Freemasonry and its Liberal continental counterpart. There appear to be very few French Masonic books available in the English language. This is unfortunate as it deprives readers who cannot read French from accessing a vast body of work and ultimately prevents us from seeing the whole picture.

Olivia Chaumount was initiated in the Parisian lodge *L'Université Maçonnique* in 1992. At that time Le Grand Orient de France did not accept women and the explanation for this apparent paradox is that in 1992 Olivia was an architect called Olivier. Fifteen years later, Olivier became Olivia and her new status as a woman was fully accepted by French law in 2008. Unfortunately, Le Grand Orient de France were not ready for this debate at that time and there was some resistance to the notion of Le Grand Orient becoming a mixed Masonic Order.

However, on 21 January 2010 the Grand Master at the time, Pierre Lambicchi, made an official pronouncement stating that Olivia Chaumont was to be considered a fully-fledged member of Le Grand Orient de France explaining that this 'did not have any repercussions on the debate regarding the freedom of each lodge to initiate or affiliate Sisters in Le Grand Orient de France.' This coincided with Masonic proceedings involving the lodge Combat in which a woman had been initiated in 2008. Four other lodges followed suit and initiated women stating that Le Grand Orient de France should not make any distinctions between genders. This caused some commotion and the initiations were deemed to be irregular and invalid. Finally, on the second of September 2010, the Assembly of Le Grand Orient de France in Vichy approved the initiation of women in the Order. There are around 2,000 women in Le Grand Orient de France at present and the number is growing. Olivia Chaumont with her brave stance, not only accelerated the initiation of women in Le Grand Orient de France something that was overdue given the fact that Le Grand Orient de France is the main exponent of Liberal Freemasonry in the world, it also advocated the importance of individual freedom. As Olivia herself said when interviewed by Colombian Freemason Ivan Michel Herrera:

*Sexual orientation is relative to individual freedom. It cannot be subjected to morality and even less declared.*

> *To have to declare it turns it into something flawed. Homosexuality isn't a defect; it is a personal orientation that finds itself in the realm of privacy. Does anyone have to declare being heterosexual?* '[14]

With 47,000 members and a history spanning three centuries Le Grand Orient de France is undoubtedly a very important part of universal Freemasonry.

I had the privilege of attending a Masonic meeting organised by Le Grand Orient de France in the beautiful Masonic temple of the hotel Andaz, in London's Liverpool Street, in January 2017. The objective of this memorable meeting was to mark the 300-year anniversary of speculative Freemasonry. It was a beautiful meeting in which approximately fifty people from eight different liberal Masonic Orders attended. I met some truly wonderful people, and realised it is for good reason that Le Grand Orient de France is the main exponent of Liberal Freemasonry in the world.

### Grande Loge de France

The Grande Loge de France traces its roots to the premier Grande Loge de France constituted in France in 1738. This is a Masonic order that could really be considered to be more a reformed regular obedience rather than a liberal one, although it is in amity with most liberal Masonic Orders. The reason for this is that Le Grande Loge de France does not accept women, rejects any political involvement and demands the presence of a Volume of the Sacred Law in each one of its meetings. Because Le Grande Loge de France split from Le Grand Orient de France in 1894 Le Grande Loge de France has never been recognised as a being 'regular' by the United Grand Lodge of England. With 900 lodges and 34,000 members it is the third largest masonic Order in France and has 23 international lodges working in 13 different countries worldwide.

Alain Graesel, the Grand Master of the Grande Loge de France defines the aims of the Grande Loge de France thus:

---

[14] Michel Herrera, I 'El Dialogo con Olivia Chaumont' Cultura Masonica issue 15, Editorial Masonica Es, Asturias (Spain) 2013

*The Grande Loge de France is an order that welcomes men from all backgrounds and beliefs who hold a common passion which is key to their project: that human beings can fully express and develop their potential. The work of the initiate is, after all, an exceptional adventure upon which the initiate's intellectual, ethical and spiritual progression rests.*[15]

## Le Droit Humain

In 1880 a number of Craft lodges broke away from the Supreme Council in France and created Le Grande Loge Symbolique Ecossaise de France. In January of 1882 a lodge belonging to the Grande Loge Symbolique Ecossaise de France, *Les Libres penseurs de Pecq,* created its own by-laws and decided to initiate, pass and raise women rights activist Maria Deraismes. This caused such tensions and criticism that many members of the lodge resigned. In 1893 with the assistance of senator and active socialist Georges Martin, seventeen women had already been raised to the third degree and on the fourth of April 1893 a new Masonic Order saw the light of day; the Grande Loge Symbolique Ecossaise Le Droit Humain which by 1901 became the International Masonic Order for Men and Women Le Droit Humain. From France the Order spread to the rest of Europe, the Americas, Africa and parts of Asia and Australasia. Today, Le Droit Humain boasts 30,000 members spread to 60 countries.

This Masonic Order was created with the sole aim of admitting women into Freemasonry in a time in which this was simply unthinkable. But who were Georges Martin and Maria Deraismes?

Georges Martin was born in 1844 into a wealthy bourgeois family in Paris. His father threw him out of the family home when Georges decided to do his secondary exams in arts and humanities and not in sciences. Georges was a resilient and hard-working young man who made his own way in life without having to resort to his family and position. He studied medicine and enlisted in Garibaldi's army and after almost a decade returned home and made peace with his father. He was initiated in 1879 and by then was very

---

[15]http://www.elcentrodelaunionescocesa.org/es/inicio/8-cat-es/articulos/12-xv-aniversario-de-la-logia-masonica-el-centro-de-la-union-escocesa

interested in the important issues of his time: laïcité, women's rights, education reforms and social security for all. He was elected Senator for the Seine in 1885, having already left his medical practice. Although a rich man by birth and thereafter through his social position, he died in poverty as he used all of his wealth and resources to establish Le Droit Humain. His wife, Marie, also remortgaged her properties for the sake of the Order and was the first female Grand Master of Le Droit Humain.

His attempts at getting Masonic Orders to accept women were met with resistance, so Georges Martin took matters into his own hands and created Le Droit Humain.

But for Martin, Freemasonry had a social mission and was not just limited to the individual pursuit of self-knowledge or moral and spiritual improvement. For him, Freemasonry had a part to play in society and perhaps even in the political realm and in this, Martin was a typical continental Freemason. Georges Martin's views on the meaning of Freemasonry were deeply steeped in his political ideals.

We can get a good idea of what Freemasonry is for Georges Martin in his definition of the institution,

*Mixed gender Freemasonry is not a new cult but a humanist philosophy that hopes to introduce its values in society. Human rights, peace between all the nations on earth, freedom, equality, fraternity: these are the precepts of mixed gender Freemasonry with which we hope to brighten justice, tolerance and solidarity.*

Georges Martin died in 1916. His work and dedication alongside Maria Deraismes in the creation of Le Droit Humain.

Maria Deraismes co-founded Le Droit Humain with Georges Martin. She too came from a wealthy middle-class family into which she was born in 1828. Deraismes studied classical languages, biblical studies and was very interested in oriental religions and philosophy. She created the Association for the Rights of Women in 1869 and shared many interests with Georges Martin such as secularism and freedom of thought. She was initiated in 1882 into *Les Libres Penseurs de Pecq* which as mentioned previously was part of Le Grande Loge Symbolique Ecossaise de France. This caused uproar and Freemasonry as a whole closed its doors to

Deraismes who spent a number of years trying to create a Masonic Order that would allow for mixed gender lodges. In 1893 with the assistance of Georges Martin she created what would later become Le Droit Humain and the rest is history. Her views on Freemasonry are remarkable and timeless:

> *Remain always united, help each other and never allow the chain of union to break. The Freemasonry that has been practised up to now belongs to the past; you my sisters will practise tomorrow's Freemasonry. I have left the Temple unfinished you must continue to work among its columns to find the rights of the whole of humankind.*

Maria Deraismes died in 1894, the same year that Le Grande Loge de France was founded. This lodge was created out of a split within Le Grand Orient de France. By the first half of the twentieth century the Order had already spread internationally from England to America and many other countries.

### Le Droit Humain in Great Britain

The British Federation of Le Droit Humain was founded by Annie Besant in 1902. Besant was, like Martin and Deraismes, a political activist who fought for freedom of conscience and women's rights. She was also a member of the Fabian society and throughout her life fought injustice. Besant supported the London match girls strike in 1888 and took part in the 1905 Bloody Sunday demonstration. She almost faced a prison sentence for writing a pamphlet advocating the use of birth control.

She married Anglican vicar Frank Besant in 1867. This was not a happy union and her husband proved to be a difficult man. Annie Besant's marriage made her question her religious beliefs and search for alternative forms of spirituality. She eventually separated from her husband, and influenced by George Bernard Shaw, joined the Fabian Society. In the 1890s she became involved in the Theosophical society and through the prominent Theosophist, Francesca Arundale, Besant became aware of Le Droit Humain. The first lodge in London was consecrated by Marie-Georges Martin. Annie Besant was initiated in 1902 in Paris and on her return to

England she was influential in spreading Co-Masonry in the United Kingdom and abroad.

A lodge was consecrated in Lahore, India, in 1904 and further lodges were consecrated in mainland Europe, Scandinavia, the US and Australia. By the 1930s the British Federation boasted a large number of lodges and members and the international order Le Droit Humain as a whole went through a period of growth and development.

The British Federation has 16 Craft lodges and a number of triangles operating in the British Isles,

To offer further insight into mixed gender lodges of the British Federation the following will be of interest:

### Lodge Golden Rule No. 21

The lodge was founded in 1905 by Annie Besant. The lodge works the *Verulam Ritual* and dedicates its work to the service of humanity following the golden rule of 'Do unto others as you would that others do unto you' Like most British Federation lodges, it meets at Hexagon House in Surbiton, Surrey the headquarters of the British Federation. Edward L. Gardner, the prominent Theosophist and esoteric writer, was a member of this lodge.

### Lodge Hermes No. 20

The lodge was founded in 1905 by astrologists Alan and Bessie Leo who also founded the London Astrological Society. The lodge works in order to understand the deeper meaning of life and to study astrology as a means to comprehend human character. This lodge meets in Surbiton.

### Lodge International Concorde No. 977

This lodge works under the motto Post Tenebras Lux and was founded in 1943 in order to accommodate who had been displaced from their countries of origin by the war. Polish officers and Tibetan Monks worked in the lodge towards their special work of international relations while London was under the attack of German air raids. This lodge meets in Surbiton and works the Georges Martin Ritual which is very similar to the Ancient and Accepted Scottish Rite practised by continental lodges in mainland Europe.

### Lodge Jupiter No. 989

This lodge's special work is the study of universal healing in the 'Light of Freemasonry.' Jupiter Lodge works the Lauderdale Ritual which is a very esoteric ritual and derives from Annie Besant's Dharma Ritual and combines elements from the Ancient and Accepted Scottish Rite and the Emulation Ritual. The Lodge was consecrated in 1948. According to their by-laws at least three 'volumes of the sacred lore' should be displayed when the lodge is working: the Bible, the Quran and the Bhagavad-gita.

### Lodge Light of Amen Ra No. 717

Under the motto 'The Light is within you. Let the Light shine' the members of this lodge dedicate their work to the study of Masonic symbolism and its direct, spiritual application to day-to-day life. The lodge was consecrated in Cambridge in 1930 but meets in Surbiton.

### Lodge Maa Kheru No. 975

The work of this lodge consists in acquiring a higher state of consciousness through the practice of Masonic Ritual. The ritual worked in this lodge is the very esoteric and spiritual Lauderdale Ritual. The meaning of Maa Kheru from the ancient Egyptian language is 'to be of true voice'. The lodge also meets in Hexagon House, in Surbiton. Christine Hartley (1897-1985) was a member of this lodge.

### Lodge Mercury No. 706

Under the motto 'Suaviter in modo, fortiter in re' this lodge aims to uphold the ancient traits of Freemasonry and express them in life. This is a lodge with a very diverse membership in which independence of thought and self-reliance are very important.

### Lodge Morning Star No. 714

At present this is the only lodge of the British Federation that meets in central London, in Notting Hill Gate. The lodge was consecrated by Arnold Banks in 1920 but went into abeyance until its revival in 2010. The special work of the lodge consists in preparing its members for 'great service'.

### Lodge Plato No. 31

This lodge was consecrated in 1908 and under the motto 'I seek the Light' it dedicates its work to 'perpetuate the Platonic principles of equality and the search for good in oneself. This lodge meets in Leeds.

### Lodge St Francis No. 817

This lodge meets at The Temple, in Tekels Park, Surrey. Its work is dedicated to serve the Head of all True Freemasons in the World and to await the revival of the Ancient Mysteries. The members of the lodge work to promote self-knowledge, spiritual harmony and ceremonial excellence.

### Lodge St Germain No. 904

The lodge is dedicated to the eighteenth century occultist Comte de St Germain, a very important figure within the British Federation and the lodge motto 'From the Unreal lead us to the Real, from Darkness to Light, from Death to Immortality' reflects the esoteric and spiritual aims of the lodge. Self-knowledge and the western mystery tradition are important aspects of the masonic work of St Germain. The lodge was consecrated in 1928 and currently meets in Surbiton (headquarters of the British Federation).

### Lodge St Michael No. 878

This lodge was consecrated in Dublin in 1928, went in abeyance for a number of years and was revived in 1987. The lodge meets at The Masonic Temple in Newtownards, County Down. It works under the motto 'Let there be Light' and its special work is the dissemination of ancient masonic ceremonial and symbolic works to future generations. This lodge works the Irish Ritual.

### Lodge St Patrick No. 879

Under the motto 'Herald the Dawn' this is the only lodge in Northern Ireland that works the Lauderdale Ritual. The lodge works towards the creation of peace and harmony through masonic ritual.

### The Scottish Lodge No. 884

This lodge's work is to research and promote ancient forms of rituals of Masonry. It was founded in 1927 by Annie Besant, went into abeyance twice being resuscitated in 1937 and more recently in

2007. It works the Scottish Ritual and its motto is 'Rise and overcome'. This is a very warm and fraternal lodge that meets in Surbiton.

### Lodge Sirius No. 704

This lodge's motto is 'I have entered in as a man of no understanding. I shall come forth in the form of a strong spirit.' The lodge meets in Tunbridge Wells.

### The Lodge Human Duty No. 6

Was founded in 1920 and it survives today as a shelter for masons who are unable to attend lodges regularly.

In addition to the above the Triangle Elizabeth Saint Leger meets in Ireland and the new lodge Y Ddraig is starting to work in Bristol. At the time of writing this book a new Triangle is now in operation in the Brighton area, including another triangle in London, Tir N'an Oige. There are also several Chapters, Consistories and Aeropages for the higher degrees.

Le Droit Humain has three main distinctive characteristics: it is a mixed Order; an international organisation and initiation is ongoing from the 1st Craft degree to the 33rd degree.

Today Le Droit Humain has around 30,000 members spread in over 60 countries. In its constitutions it defines itself as an initiatory, philosophical, philanthropic and secular institution with the mission of working towards the progress and perfection of humanity. The International headquarters of the order are in Paris and at the time of writing this book the current Grand Master of the order is Daniel Bolens.

# CHAPTER 5: The uses of Freemasonry

## Political Freemasonry

We have seen in the section dedicated to Le Grand Orient de France that when a Masonic Order makes incursions into the realm of politics, the results can be unfortunate. There have been of course flagrant cases of corruption such as the scandal of the lodge P2 in Italy, which allegedly counted among its members former Italian premier Silvio Berlusconi and was supposedly involved with the mafia and the mysterious murder of banker Roberto Calvi in London. As recently as 2013 there was a scandal involving Jerome Cahuzac, finance minister and Freemason who was accused of committing tax fraud and although this was down to the minister, as an individual and arguably had nothing to do with Freemasonry it fuelled anti masonic speculation, The worst scandal, which resulted in the near-annihilation of a Masonic Order, occurred within the only masonic Order in France recognised by the United Grand Lodge of England, namely the Grande Loge Nationale Française.

In 2009, François Stifani, the Grand Master of Le Grande Loge Nationale Française was taken to court by several members of his organisation over the expenditure of millions of Euros on political subscriptions. Stifani openly – and while wearing his Grand Master's hat – supported political candidate Nicolas Sarkozy, a flagrant breach of Anderson's Constitution and Masonic regularity which caused the United Grand Lodge of England to suspend its recognition of Le Grande Loge Nationale Française in 2012. Le Grande Loge Nationale Française then split as a large number of members deeply unhappy about these developments left the Order to found a separate Masonic jurisdiction.

The key issue is for Freemasons to be able to deal with general, universal topics such as Justice, Freedom, Equality and so forth without ever aligning oneself, as a Freemason belonging to a Masonic Order, to any given political party. Furthermore, it is essential that any political views are individual and not institutional.

In French Freemasonry, with its insistence on laïcité and left-wing politics this can be a difficult balance to strike.

In his article *'Us and the Crisis'*[16] Spanish Freemason Juan Alberdi disagrees with the landmark forbidding political discussion in the lodge which he sees as an extension of the prohibition to discuss religious topics. Rather vexed, Juan Alberdi asks:

*As a consequence of this prohibition [to discuss politics in lodge] must we remain silent before grave social and political problems? Must we limit ourselves to the usual rhetoric platitude of the Declaration of Human Rights and other similar statements this is to a mere catalogue of good intentions?*

For Alberdi Freemasonry is 'not only a method of personal self-improvement it's the metaphor of the polished cubic stone as part of a bigger building.'

This is a compelling argument. Freemasonry should be of benefit to the world at large. Organisations such as the United Grand Lodge in the UK and its counterparts in the United States, for example, do incredible work in the way of charity. However, smaller orders do not necessarily have the funds or infrastructure to follow suit. As Alberdi points out, involvement, or at the very least discussion of social and political issues might be a way to do this. For me, perhaps because of my past in 'regular' Freemasonry or simply because I do not like mixing politics with spirituality and I see Freemasonry mainly as a secular spiritual system, Freemasonry's work is to help us find out who we are and to connect with the Transcendence and improve as human beings. I do not believe that this should entail tackling political issues as Freemasons but rather as individuals. The institution should not be hijacked by political discourse. If it does, then how is it to be a free space for debate, a place in which to unite 'that which has been dispersed?' Pluralism can only be guaranteed when politics and religion are taken out of the agenda. Freemasonry has different objectives and should rise above political and religious narratives.

On the European continent – in Spain and France in particular – it is quite natural to see Freemasons marching to

---

[16]Masoneria y Politica, Cultura Masonica Editorial Masonica, Asturias (Spain) 2013

support abortion, secularism and also to honour military and political figures on the political left from the twentieth century. Some of these ideals of progress seem to be stuck in the time machine and hark back to the leftism of the 1930s, which in my opinion has no relevance whatsoever in Freemasonry. I am not saying that these ideals are good or bad, this is not the point, but Freemasonry must remain apolitical.

It is my belief each person should have the right to express their beliefs as they see fit. However, when that particular belief is executed under the umbrella of Freemasonry, (be it a member acting outside of Freemasonry as a Freemason) the consequences to the collective Fraternity can be detrimental, since Freemasonry works as a collective organisation – the one action affecting the all.

Needless to say, each Freemason should do as he or she pleases to support their beliefs but this should be on a personal and individual level.

### Esoteric Freemasonry

Firstly, it is essential that we explain what the term 'esoteric' means. It is a word that is often misused and misunderstood but all that it really means is 'hidden or concealed knowledge' as opposed to exoteric which means 'knowledge known to or understood by the majority.' Within Freemasonry an interpretation of esoteric, could mean the discovery of certain truths about the initiate and the world around him or her. Masonic symbolism is open and cannot be pinned down and it is herein that Freemasonry remains vibrant and relevant. It is for this reason politics, religion or dogma of any sort should not ever taint Freemasonry.

Masonic symbolism points the candidate for initiation towards a wide range of truths about the human condition and the world: birth, life and death, God or the Transcendence and all the unexplained questions of life. The most popular analogy employed in Freemasonry is the one of the Freemason polishing the 'excrescences' that protrude from his or her 'stone', the rough Ashlar, until it is turned into a perfect cubic stone fit to be inserted into the Temple of Humanity. Masonic method demands that the candidate challenges his beliefs and fears and embarks on a quest for individuation and self-knowledge.

A Masonic lodge with its strange rituals and ceremonies is a perfect space where these questions about life, the human condition and the world can be asked. The hidden truths, the secrets, are to be found within the heart of each individual Freemason, and are personal and non-transferable. There are no other secrets, no conspiracies and certainly no material gain to be obtained in Freemasonry.

But there is another layer of meaning attached to the term esoteric; the fact that Freemasonry is part of the Western mystery tradition, that is, a line of thought that has always run parallel to the mainstream but where freedom, creativity and a desire to see things in a different light has always been present. In this sense I am using the word esotericism to mean precisely what academics refer to as the Western mystery tradition.

There is a 'Golden Thread' running through a number of systems of thoughts, religions and secret societies which starts in late antiquity with Hermetic philosophy and the Corpus Hermeticum allegedly written by Hermes Trismegistus, who is thought to be an incarnation of the god Thoth and the Greek god Hermes. The text dates to the second century AD and copies of the manuscript resurfaced in the fifteenth century and were translated by humanist, scholar and Catholic priest Marsilio Ficino (1433-1499). *The Corpus Hermeticum*, on one level, discusses the great themes of humanity, such as the immortality of the soul, the universe and the human mind. But on another level the syncretistic character of the text and the absence of a dogmatic approach made it very appealing to the Renaissance man who was looking for alternatives to the religious scholasticism of the Catholic Church. It is striking that although the Corpus Hermeticum is a spiritual, quasi magical wisdom book parts of it were used by Renaissance philosopher Pico della Mirandola (1463-1494) in his famous *Oration for the Dignity of Man*: 'A great miracle, Asclepius, is the human being'.

Another ancient strand of this Golden Thread is Gnosticism, a set of religious beliefs and systems which originated in the Mediterranean and Middle East in the first century AD. These survive today with Gnostic groups such as the Mandaeans as well as some more recent Gnostic sects. Gnosticism, from the word 'Gnosis' (knowledge) can be loosely described as the belief that this world has been created by a false and imperfect god, the Demiurge, that man has been separated from the divine and that he is trapped in the prison of matter. Through a specific knowledge of the workings of the cosmos and a divine spark contained within him he will be able to transcend the world of flesh and matter and reach the real God.

Both Hermetic thought and Gnosticism are linked to the Ancient mystery religions practised in antiquity predominantly by Romans, Greeks and the Ancient Egyptians before them and in which long and convoluted initiatory ceremonies were performed following magical thinking. Centuries later in the late Middle Ages and the Renaissance, Alchemy, the Jewish Cabbala and Astrology as well as Magic were pursued by a number of personalities seeking an alternative source of knowledge. Freemasonry is part of this tradition although I have to make it very clear that I do not believe for a moment in a linear connection between the mysteries or Gnosticism and Freemasonry, rather that all three movements share this desire to stand aside from the mainstream and to think things again, differently.

### Philosophical Freemasonry

This particular way of focusing on the masonic work and method sometimes merges with the political approach, also called humanist or rationalist, but I think that there is a case for putting philosophical Freemasonry in its own category. There are lodges – rather Grand Lodges or Grand Orients at large, since each lodge in every obedience has its own by-laws and culture – which will be very careful to subscribe to the ancient landmark of 'no politics.'

Philosophical Freemasons will explore Freemasonry and its symbols from a rationalistic point of view and focus mainly on the philosophers of the Enlightenment and ultimately on philosophy as a whole. For these philosophical Freemasons, Freemasonry is an intellectual process, a free-thinking space whereby the exploration of wider questions regarding humankind and philosophy enquiry are able to be discussed. Philosophical, or rationalist Freemasons look at Freemasonry as a method with which to fend off intellectual inertia and constantly challenge sets of beliefs and generate new ideas. Pieces of architecture or *planches* are therefore of vital importance in these lodges. Hegel, Kant, Hume and Berkeley will be no doubt cited frequently in these works but also will Nietzsche,

Wittgenstein and postmodern thinkers. Art, Humanities and other fields of culture will be discussed also and in order to picture what a philosophical lodge might look like one only had to think about what the coffee houses and saloons of the eighteenth century must have been like.

# CHAPTER 6: Universalism

### The Appeal of Strasbourg

Regular Freemasonry has its 'Holy See' in England, in the shape of the United Grand Lodge of England; a self-appointed masonic regulatory body in amity with all regular Masonic Orders in the world that fully subscribe to the ancient landmarks as set out by the United Grand Lodge of England. This gives Regular Freemasonry a seemingly international indissolubility and unity.

What about Liberal Freemasonry? Does Liberal Freemasonry have something equivalent, a unifying body at an international level?

On 21 January 1961 twelve Masonic Orders led by Le Grand Orient de France made what is known as the Appeal of Strasbourg in an attempt at 'restoring the chain of union' with the hope of uniting Freemasonry around a set of common ideals while at the same time upholding the diversity, sovereignty and by-laws of every member organization. This act will lead to the creation of CLIPSAS (The Centre of Liaison and Information of Masonic Powers Signatories of Strasbourg Appeal).

### The Appeal of Strasbourg States the Following Principles as its Objectives:

- 'To restore the chain of union severed by the unfortunate exclusivity of some orders contrary to the principles of the Anderson Constitutions of 1723

- 'That it is therefore convenient to start again as a community considering each and every tradition, rites, symbols and beliefs framed by a respect for the absolute freedom of conscience and to determine the conditions that qualify a Freemason'

- 'Working to the Glory of the Great Architect of the Universe and request that one of the three Great Lights is a sacred book is something that should be left to each lodge and obedience to decide'

- 'To establish fraternal relations and open the doors of the Temple to every Freemason, man or woman, who has received the Light in a perfect and just Lodge on condition that the regulations of the lodge allow this without the requirement of reciprocity'

What is a 'Just and Perfect' Lodge according to the masonic Orders that founded CLIPSAS? The website for CLIPSAS[17] provides a very clear definition:

1. It must be formed for at least seven Freemasons
2. Three direct it, five illumine it and seven make it just and perfect
3. The lodge will work following a ritual based on the building symbolism
4. Meetings will take place in a closed and tyled space in which the following must be present: the columns J and B; the three Great Lights among which the Square and Compasses must be found; the regalia and furniture of the degree being worked and the chequered pavement.
5. The Lodge must work the degrees of Entered Apprentice, Fellow Craft and Master Mason.
6. The initiation to the degree of Entered Apprentice which takes place under the sign of the Triangle encompasses the Chamber of Reflection, the Trials and the move from Darkness to Light. The passing to the degree of Fellow Craft will take place beneath the Light of the Blazing Star. The rising of the Master Mason will entail the communication of the Hiramic legend. Each degree has its own obligations.
7. A Freemason, man or woman, is somebody who has been initiated in a Just and Perfect Lodge.

---

[17]CLIPSAS website:http://clipsas.news/?lang=en

CLIPSAS is a reaction, a natural reaction against the perceived 'rule' of Regular Freemasonry. The problem is that in spite of its desire to be inclusive it does somehow, to a much lesser extent, make the same mistake as Regular Freemasonry. Regular lodges would not necessarily pass the 'Just and Perfect' test since there are no Chambers of Reflection in English Regular lodges. In spite of this there is no doubt that CLIPSAS was a fantastic initiative and has provided Liberal Freemasonry with a degree of unity and set the basis for inter-visitation and cooperation between many liberal masonic Orders throughout the world. Many if not most liberal masonic Orders allow regular masons to visit their lodges even if these have to do it clandestinely and without being able to return the masonic welcome in their own regular lodges.

At present, (according to the CLIPSAS website admissions), there are over 70 Masonic Orders throughout the world subscribed to the organization.

- Grand Orient de France
- Grand Orient de Belgique
- Gran Loggia d'Italia
- Grand Orient de Suisse
- Grand Orient de Luxembourg
- Serenísima Gran Logia de Lengua Española
- Grand Lodge of Denmark
- Gran Logia Mixta de Puerto Rico
- George Washington Union
- Grand Rite Malgache
- Omega Grand Lodge of the State of New York
- Grande Loge Unie du Cameroun
- Fédération Française de l'Ordre Maç.·. Mixte International
- Gran Logia Simbólica Española
- Grand Orient du Congo
- Grande Loge Mixte de France
- Grande Loge Féminine de Belgique
- Grande Loge Mixte des Pays-Bas
- Grande Mixte Universelle
- Grande Oriente Lusitano

- Grande Loge Haïtienne de Saint-Jean des Ord'Outre Mer
- HUMANITAS - Freimaurergrossloge für Frauen und Männer in Deutschland
- Grande Loge de Haïti
- Gran Oriente Latino Americano
- Grand Bénin de la République du Bénin
- Großloge Humanitas Austria
- Grand Orient & Loges Associés du Congo
- Grande Loge Liberale de Turquie
- Gran Logia Mixta de Chile
- Grande Loge Française de Memphis-Misraïm
- Grande Loge Féminine de Memphis-Misraïm
- Grande Eburnie
- Grande Loge Féminine de Turquie
- Gran Logia Femenina de Chile
- Gran Loggia Massonica Femminile d'Italia
- Grande Loja Unida do Paraná
- Séréníssime Grand Orient de Grèce
- Grande Loge de la Caraïbe
- Grande Loge Nationale du Canada
- Grande Oriente Nacional "Gloria do Ocidente" do Brasil
- Gran Logia del Norte de Colombia
- Grande Loja Maçônica Mista do Brasil
- Ordre Maçonnique International DELPHI
- Grande Loge Centrale du Liban
- Grand Orient Mixte de Grèce
- Grande Loja Unida de Pernambuco
- Grande Loge Mixte de Memphis-Misraïm
- Gran Logia Central de Colombia
- Grande Loge de Cèdres
- Grande Loge Symbolique Masculine d'Afrique
- Grand Rite Malagasy Féminin
- Gran Logia Femenina de Argentina
- Gran Oriente de Chile
- Grande Loja Arquitetos de Aquário – GLADA
- Grande Loge Bet-El

- Grande Loge Féminine de Roumanie
- Gran Logia Benjamim Herrera
- Grande Loge Indépendante et Souveraine des Rites Unis
- Gran Oriente de la Francmasonería Mixta Universal
- Grande Loge du Maroc
- Gran Logia Constitucional del Perú
- Gran Oriente Federal de la Republica Argentina
- Gran Oriente de El Salvador
- Gran Logia Hiram Habif
- Gran Oriente de Roumanie
- Gran Loge Nationale Unie de Roumanie
- Federación Colombiana de Logias Masónicas
- Grande Loja Feminina do Brasil
- Grande Loge de Belgique
- Orient de Catalunya
- Gran Logia Soberana de Libres y Aceptados Masones de Venezuela
- Gran Logia Oriental del Perú
- Grande Loge Unie Du Liban
- Lithos – Fédéracion de Loges – Belgique
- Grande Loge Liberale d´Autriche
- Gran Oriente Ibérico
- Gran Oriente Ecuatoriano Nueva Era
- Grande Lodge Mixte Souveraine de France
- Grande Lodge Travaillant au Rite Ecossais Primitif Universal
- Grand Lodge of Bulgaria
- Grande Lodge des Cultures et de la Spiritualité Ordre Initiatique et Traditionnel de l'Art Royal

In addition to CLIPSAS and until 2010, the International Secretariat of the Masonic Adogmatic Powers (SIMPA) encompassed a number of international liberal masonic Orders with similar aims to those espoused by CLIPSAS. In 2010 the organization went into abeyance and the member bodies merged with CLIPSAS.

The Second Grand Principle, derived from the first, is Relief of Suffering; firstly as far as possible to harm no living being, and secondly to give aid to those who are in distress.

Another important organisation of liberal Masonic Orders still in existence today is CATENA which was founded in 1961 and accepts only member organisations which require the acknowledgement of a Supreme Being for membership.

### Listed Below are the Basic Principles Which CATENA Follow:

- The foundation of Universal Freemasonry is the acknowledgement of a Supreme Reality in which we live and move and which is the reason for our being.

- The First Grand Principle derived from this primal truth is the fundamental unity and equality of all human beings, expressed in Freemasonry as Brotherly Love, which springs from recognition of our spiritual kinship.

- The Second Grand Principle, derived from the first, is Relief of Suffering; firstly as far as possible to harm no living being, and secondly to give aid to those who are in distress.

- The Third Grand Principle is Truth, which is to have a free mind and to see things as they truly are without bias. This Principle especially relates to self-knowledge as unveiled to a mason.[18]

### CATENA has the Following Masonic Orders Amongst its Members:

---

[18] https://www.catena.org/about-catena/basic-principles/

- Humanitas—Freimaurergroßloge für Frauen und Männer in Deutschland
- Großloge Humanitas (Austria)
- The Order of Ancient Free Masonry for Men and Women (UK)
- Groupement Maconnique de Loges mixtes et independantes (France)
- Grand Loge "Humanitas Bohemia" (Czech Republic)
- Maçons Lliures Mare Nostrum (Spain)
- Romanian Masonic Mixed Order (Romania)

# CONCLUSION

*'O Sovereign and Most Worshipful of all Masters, who, in Thy infinite love and wisdom, hast devised our Order as a means to draw Thy children nearer Thee, and hast so ordained its Officers that they are emblems of Thy sevenfold power;*

*Be Thou unto us an Outer Guard, and defend us from the perils that beset us when we turn from that which is without to that which is within; Be Thou unto us an Inner Guard, and preserve our souls that desire to pass within the portal of Thy holy mysteries;*

*Be unto us the Younger Deacon, and teach our wayward feet the true and certain steps upon the path that leads to Thee: Be Thou also the Elder Deacon, and guide us up the steep and winding stairway to Thy throne;*

*Be unto us the Lesser Warden, and in the meridian sunlight of our understanding speak to us in sacraments that shall declare the splendours of Thy unmanifested light;*

*Be Thou also unto us the Greater Warden, and in the awful hour of disappearing light, when vision fails and thought has no more strength, be with us still, revealing to us, as we may bear them, the hidden mysteries of Thy shadow;*

*And so, through light and darkness, raise us, Great Master, till we are made one with Thee, in the unspeakable glory of Thy presence in the East.*
*So mote it be.'*

The Wilmhurst Prayer (a Prayer at Lodge Closing).

What we can see from the previous chapter is the extent into which Freemasonry is fragmented: there are so called regular orders that do not allow women and atheists and forbid political and religious discussion in their lodges and that do not recognise any other form of Freemasonry. There are Orders which may accept women but require a belief in a Supreme Being and there are other masonic Orders which accept women and atheists but do not allow political or religious discussion and so on. This pluralism is good in many ways as it allows a degree of freedom and tolerance but perhaps does not work well for Freemasonry as a whole keeping it divided. The universalism so boldly proclaimed by, to paraphrase the words of Alain de Keghel in his book *Freemasonry a Geopolitical Perspective,* is compromised by the intolerance of some orders and this tendency to split and fragment so common in liberal masonic Orders.

Freemasonry no longer has the influence it once had in spite of the multitude of conspiracy books full of nonsense that can be found in the bargain section of bookshops.

A long line of illustrious politicians, American presidents, scientists, thinkers, military figures and writers have been Freemasons. Although it would be a mistake to believe that America was created as some kind of Masonic project, the influence that Freemasonry has had on this noble nation is irrefutable. In the United Kingdom and during the nineteenth century Freemasonry was an important part of the British Empire spreading alongside it over the four quarters of the globe. Today it has successfully survived Tony Blair's witch hunt of the 1990s and the United Grand Lodge of England has celebrated – among many other Masonic Orders throughout the world, regular or liberal – the three hundredth anniversary of speculative Freemasonry.

In spite of the alleged apolitical character of Regular English Freemasonry this Order cannot escape the fact that it does subscribe itself to a particular model of nationalistic Freemasonry, upholds the British Monarchy and in spite of the bad press and the witch hunts has always been aligned with the establishment. Regular Freemasonry always sells itself as the mainstream, the largest and most extended model of Freemasonry and of course it is absolutely true that Regular Freemasonry has the biggest presence in the world. But it isn't all as clear cut as that, as Roger Dachez and Alain Bauer explain:

*'Nevertheless, compared to the international context, French Freemasonry is in a strong position. At its 1950s peak American Freemasonry had almost four million brothers, but had hardly more than two million at the*

*start of the 2000s only a small percentage of whom were still active. British Masonry had almost a million members but has less than five hundred thousand today. In contrast, in France, Belgium and the eastern countries there is still a strong dynamic. Today there are almost 150,000 brothers and sisters in the French mainland and overseas territories out of a total of 2.5 or 3 million Masons in the world, with the traditional Anglo-Saxon strongholds falling inexorably'* [19]

Regular Freemasonry is in decline and there are plenty of articles, blogs and podcasts by regular masons providing tips on how to retain membership. In the United States the emergence of the so-called Traditional Observance Lodges in which high standards of ritual ceremony, formalism and the application and study of Masonic symbolism might be the way forward but Regular Freemasonry risks losing its touch and relevance unless it is willing to adapt and make some compromises. The United Grand Lodge of England has remedied this by revamping their website, becoming attuned to new technologies and through a general process of openness and transparency in order to attract young men into its ranks. But it is still a sad state of affairs that well-established Orders such as Le Droit Humain, Le Grand Orient of France and many others throughout the world are not recognised by the United Grand Lodge of England.

Liberal Freemasonry with its splits and divisions has also failed in a way to maintain a united front. In my personal opinion its incursions into politics are flawed and irrelevant and aligned with a misguided leftism that belongs to the twentieth century and has no relevance today. Although there is truth in the fact that Freemasonry in the eighteenth century contributed positively to the creation of modernity and helped western societies move from feudalism to modernity it should not be considered a kind of Church of the Republic in the same way that it should not be a mere extension of the Establishment. Freemasonry should go beyond all that: it should be a distinct organisation applying its own values and leaving its

---

[19]Dachez, R Freemasonry a French view, Policy Studies Organisation, Westphalia Press, France 2015

members to express their own individual political and religious beliefs in their private lives. The truth is that humanist Masonic Orders, with their attachment to human dignity and theist Masonic Orders with their spiritual and moral objectives are both ultimately sharing the same goals and aspirations.

Freemasonry as a whole has failed to uphold the very premises of universalism it created. It has failed to self-apply its own ideals and one would hope that one day in the not very distant future all Masonic Orders will at the very least recognise each other and allow inter-visitation. This could be done without compromising landmarks or traditions.

But for all its faults, Freemasonry constitutes an extraordinary attempt to create a universal fraternity of men and women, an alternative form of spirituality and human intellect. Institutions such as the UNITED NATIONS, UNESCO, AMNESTY INTERNATIONAL, JUSTICE UNIVERSAL, RED CROSS and the EUROPEAN UNION resonate strongly with Masonic ideals.

If Freemasonry were a living being and had goals and aspirations, the twentieth century would have been its biggest and most ambitious dream. Some questions to contemplate:
What does the future hold? What is the role of Freemasonry in the twenty-first century? Has Freemasonry a role to play, directly or indirectly, in world affairs, or should it be a form of secular spirituality and an open but personal space for philosophical and intellectual debate?

Needless to say, I fully respect all the different perspectives on Freemasonry and see the fraternity's objectives as being a personal path to intellectual, spiritual and moral self-development which will lead each individual Freemason to become freer, more tolerant and more aware. It is then that each individual Freemason will be able to enrich the world in his or her own particular way. But for this we must go back to basics: if Freemasonry is still relevant today this is due to the freedom and creativity that its symbols and allegories afford us. The truth and relevance of Freemasonry rests on its symbols and rituals and in the manner in which Freemasonry can create free thinking individuals who are not afraid to meet and mix with others who may have different political and religious beliefs.

This tolerance and respect are essential in the twenty-first century, a period in which we are seeing an increasing rise in intolerance and materialism.

If some of the criticisms above seem a bit harsh, I must clarify that it was well meant as constructive criticism. On a personal level I can only say good things about Freemasonry, but of course as any human institution, it is not perfect and one of its biggest problems is that in spite of advocating universal fraternal values it is deeply fragmented and divided. Freemasonry has allowed me to negotiate my spirituality and has provided me with the opportunity to write, which has been a lifelong vocation of mine. I have met some wonderful people thanks to Freemasonry, whom I would otherwise never have met in my day-to-day life. I have also received support in times of difficulty. Above all, Freemasonry has inculcated in me the value of tolerance and respect and for this I am most grateful to this institution.

Ultimately, leaving aside all the intellectual and philosophical baggage, Freemasonry is about people, it is about friendship and a commitment to matter to others and also to care about them.

Let us hope that one day, in the not too distant future, the Chain of Union will be restored and that Freemasonry will stand united to promote its values.

## ABOUT THE AUTHOR

Darren is a Freemason and was a member of the United Grand Lodge from 2006-2014 and joined the British Federation of the International Order of Freemasonry for Men and Women Le Droit Humain in 2016 and is currently a member.

Born in London in 1972, he was raised in Spain where he lived until 1998. He returned to London and read English at London Metropolitan University (previously known as the University of North London).

He is a published author, *More Light: Today's Freemasonry for Men and-Women* (2017) co-authored with Julian Rees.

Darren is a prolific writer on the subject of Freemasonry in both English and Spanish, and has written for the Spanish website Masonería Española; for *The Freemason* (the digital magazine of the British Federation of Le Droit Humain) and has also written a number of essays for the prestigious masonic website Pietre Stones Review of Freemasonry. Darren has also appeared in Podcast interviews with the celebrated podcast AEON GNOSTIC BYTES.

# APPENDIX 1

## A Note on Ritual

There are countless rituals employed by the many different Masonic Orders and jurisdictions that operate throughout the world but I will briefly discuss some of the main ones in use today. It is important to note that a Rite is a collection of degrees or so-called Side Orders and a ritual is the particular ceremonial working employed in a given degree so to provide an example the Ancient and Accepted Scottish Rite encompasses 33 degrees whereas the Emulation Ritual or the Lauderdale Ritual are worked only in the three Craft degrees of Entered Apprentice, Fellow Craft and Master Mason.

## The Emulation Ritual

The Emulation ritual is not a Rite or system of degrees but it is a very important masonic ritual used by the vast majority of lodges working under the auspices of the United Grand Lodge of England, the 'Holy See' of Masonic regularity throughout the world.

This ritual was created by the Lodge of Reconciliation in 1813 shortly before the union of the Moderns and the Ancients which resulted, ultimately, in the creation of the United Grand Lodge of England. The standards of ritual work are maintained by the Emulation Lodge of Improvement which was founded in 1823 and still operates to this day ensuring that the ritual is memorized and that no changes are made to it. Many regular Masonic Orders appoint visiting officers to inspect lodge meetings and ensure that no deviations from the ritual and Masonic regular practice are taking place.

The Emulation Ritual is very subtle, perhaps closer in its form to the Ancient Charges. It has many different variants (called 'workings') such as the Taylor's ritual, the Logic ritual and the West End ritual to name but a few. All these rituals are approved by the United Grand Lodge of England and the differences between them are minimal. Emulation is the premier ritual used in British regular Freemasonry and has a set of distinctive features:

- The ritual makes clear references to prayer and to the Godhead throughout.

- The offices of the Senior and Junior Deacons are an important feature of the degree: the Junior Deacon accompanies the candidate during the perambulations of the first degree and the Senior Deacon does the same in the second degree. They are both responsible for "carrying all messages and communications" from the Senior and Junior Wardens and they also arrange the tracing board.

- The tracing board: These boards are often beautiful works of art depicting the particular symbols of the degree they represent. There is one for each degree and the relevant board must be displayed during the meeting.

- The offices are progressive and rotate annually or biannually so an Entered Apprentice typically sits in the Worshipful Master's Chair after seven years and having gone through all the offices of the lodge: Inner Guard, Junior Deacon, Senior Deacon, Junior Warden and Senior Warden. Once the Worshipful Master has served his term he becomes a Past Master for another year or two and then might fill one of the non-progressive offices, Director of Ceremonies, Secretary, Treasurer and so on.

- There are no pieces of architecture but a number of approved lectures can be read in open lodge.

- Typically, the first three degrees of symbolic or Craft Freemasonry are separate and independent and any other Masonic degrees are considered side orders. In Great Britain the vast majority of who have completed their third degree will go on to join a Royal Arch Chapter and a system of side degrees called the York Rite which includes degrees such as the Mark Mason degree, the Royal and Select Masters, Knights Templar and so on. The Ancient and Accepted Scottish Rite in Great Britain – known as the Ancient and Accepted Rite for England and Wales – operates as a different organisation and accepts all 'regularly' initiated Master Masons who join the 18th

Degree, referred to as Rose Croix, after having received in name only the degrees from the 4th to the 17th separately.

## The Ancient and Accepted Scottish Rite

The Ancient and Accepted Scottish Rite is a system of degrees which is used by many continental Masonic Orders but also by most American Regular Grand Lodges. It is worth noting that due to historical developments American Grand Lodges in amity with the United Grand Lodge of England use the Ancient and Accepted Scottish Rite, so to say that Regular Lodges use the Emulation ritual and Liberal Lodges the Ancient and Accepted Scottish Rite would be incorrect but it is important to point out that most Liberal Orders in France, Spain, England, Italy and other European countries do use the Ancient and Accepted Scottish Rite.

According to legend the Rite was created during the time of the Crusades to resurface in the eighteenth century. Some modern theories suggest that when the Master of the Knights Templar Order was burnt at the stake many of his men escaped to Scotland where they were given refuge by local operative lodges of. This is of course mere speculation and there is no solid evidence that can validate these theories but at any rate it may explain the penchant of the Ancient and Accepted Scottish Rite for chivalric symbolism.

The Rite works the first three degrees of Entered Apprentice, Fellow Craft and Master Mason in a Craft or Symbolic lodge in the same way as other Masonic rites but the 4th up to the 33rd degrees are worked in lodges of perfection, Chapters and Aeropagus administered by an independent Supreme Council.

The Chevalier Ramsay created the first lodge of perfection in Bordeaux in 1744 which was the beginning of the AASR. From France it made its way to America where it met with great success partly because of its European, historical flavour but also, perhaps, as a particular Masonic ritual that would distinguish American masons from their British foes. The Ancient and Accepted Scottish Rite was further developed in the United States by Albert Pike (1809-1891) journalist, writer, lawyer and Confederate officer.

## The degrees of the Rite are as follows:

*Lodge of Perfection or ineffable degrees*
4-Secret Master
5-Perfect Master
6-Intimate Secretary
7-Provost and Judge
8-Intendant of the Building
9-Elu of the Nine
10-Elu of the Fifteen
11-Sublime Master Elect
12-Grand Master Architect
13-Knight of the Royal Arch
14-Perfect Elu or Grand Elect Mason

*Council of Princes of Jerusalem*
15-Knight of the East or Knight of the Sword
16-Prince of Jerusalem

*Rose Croix Chapter*
17-Knight of the East and West
18-Sovereign Prince Rosecroix or Knight of the Pelican and Eagle

*Consistory of Princes of the Royal Secret*
19-Grand Pontiff
20-Grand Master ad vitam
21-Noachite Patriarch or Prussian Knight
22-Prince of Lebanon or Knight of the Royal Axe
23- Chief of the Tabernacle
24-Prince of the Tabernacle
25-Knight of the Brazen Serpent
26- Prince of Mercy or Scottish Trinitarian
27- Knight of the Sun or Prince Adept
28- Knight Commander of the Temple
29- Scottish Knight of St Andrew
30- Grand Elected Knight Kadosh or Knight of the White and Black Eagle

31- Inspector Inquisitor Commander
32- Sublime Prince of the Royal Secret
33- Sovereign Grand Inspector General

*(The last degree is conferred by the Supreme Council of the 33rd degree).*

The list of degrees given above reflects the most common degrees worked but there are different workings of the Ancient and Accepted Scottish Rite. The higher degrees are normally progressive and not considered side orders. There are no deacons in this rite but it is worth remembering that there are also variants of the Ancient and Accepted Scottish Rite as for example, the Lauderdale Ritual which is worked exclusively by Le Droit Humain and incorporates elements from the Emulation ritual.

Typically a lodge working the Ancient and Accepted Scottish Rite does not have the Junior and Senior Deacon offices but the office of the Brother Expert and Brother Orator are introduced. The former is the equivalent of the Director of Ceremonies in Emulation and the latter is an office unique to the Rite; the Brother Orator acts as a representation of masonic law and perhaps in that sense could be equated to the figure of the Visiting Officer in Regular English Freemasonry.

The first three degrees worked in the Ancient and Accepted Scottish Rite differ greatly from how they are worked in Emulation. It is in the Ancient and Accepted Scottish Rite that elements such as the Chamber of Reflection, the Cup of Libations and the Trials of earth, air, water and fire are introduced. In these three first degrees masonic lectures (called Pieces of Architecture) are presented and debated. The ritual is designed to shake up the candidate making use of certain actions and props which have the ultimate aim of awakening the candidate from his 'profane' life as opposed to the Emulation ritual which operates in a more subtle, understated manner.

The Ancient and Accepted Scottish Rite is used in American Regular Freemasonry and in other regular Masonic Orders throughout the world but as mentioned previously the vast majority of liberal Orders in Europe and beyond use this ritual too.

## The French Rite

Known as the most secular of all Masonic Rites this ritual derives from the English Modern rite. In 1877, when the Grand Orient of France decided to eliminate the requisite for the belief in a Supreme Being and the immortality of the soul, the Masonic ritual was adjusted severely and in 1879 all religious references removed. Louis Amiable (1837-1897) who was a lawyer and a prominent Freemason and member of the French College of Rites revised the ritual further in 1886 influenced by the emerging positivism of the time. The Rite was modified again in 1938 by Arthur Groussier (1863-1957) a member of the Revolutionary Socialist Workers party and also a prominent member of Le Grand Orient de France. By the time Groussier was in a position to modify the ritual, the positivism and rationalist fervour of the late nineteenth century was in decline and Groussier modified the ritual to reflect the renewed interest of many in Masonic symbolism. French journalist and art critic René Guilly (1921-1992) attempted to further imbue the rite with symbolism and a more esoteric character and created the Traditional French Rite based on it.

The Rite works the three Craft degrees of Entered Apprentice, Fellow craft and Master Mason and the degrees of Secret Elect, Scottish Grand Elect, Knight of the Orient, Sovereign Rose Croix, Perfect Freemason and Grand Commander of the Temple.

## Lauderdale Ritual

This ritual is not a mainstream ritual and as far as I am aware it is only used by some Federations of Le Droit Humain, mainly in English speaking countries and perhaps by some other Co-Masonic Orders that were created as the result of splits within Le Droit Humain. The Lauderdale ritual is a very interesting and unique ritual that combines some elements of Emulation and the Scottish Rite as well as some unique elements of its own. This ritual was created by Annie Besant herself in 1904 although it was known at the time as the Dharma Ritual. When the ritual was reprinted in 1992 it was renamed 'Lauderdale' because the headquarters of the British Federation of Le Droit Humain had been originally located in Lauderdale Road before moving to Ladbroke Terrace. The headquarters of the British Federation at the time of writing this book are located in Surbiton.

Because of what has been called the 'Besant Accord' lodges using the Lauderdale ritual work, *To the Glory of the Great Architect of the Universe* and currently the triple option is available to members, namely, working to the glory of the Great Architect of the Universe or to the Perfection of Humanity or to both.

The British Federation of Le Droit Humain differs from other Federations, perhaps because of the spiritual character of the founders of the British Federation many of whom were Theosophists but possibly, also because of the influence of English regular Freemasonry. The approach is however inclusive and tolerant, as Claude Voileau and Brian Roberts explain in their essay *The Lauderdale Ritual:*

> *In the preface of the 1992 Ritual we can read: "As Masons may belong to any religion, it is desirable to have on the Altar, a Scripture of more than one Great Faith, but no attempt should be made to impose any particular interpretation of the Ritual upon any Brother of the Order. The Lodges should observe towards each other the old rule: 'In things essential, Unity; in non-essential, Liberty; in all things, Charity'.*[20]

The Lauderdale ritual focuses its work on the spiritual development of the candidate through the use of masonic symbolism. In my opinion this ritual has the best parts of the Emulation Ritual – the obligations and the high ceremonial standard – and the Scottish rite; the elementals, the three symbolic journeys as well as its own particularities such as the fact that gloves are not always used or, more importantly perhaps, the office of the Thurifer who cleanses the Temple with incense at the opening of the lodge.

---

[20] Voileau C and Roberts B, Le Droit Humain Bulletin Number 50, April 2017

# APPENDIX 2

## Javier Otaola Former President of CLIPSAS 1997-2000

Javier Otaola Bajeneta was born in Bilbao, in Spain's Basque country in 1956. He works as a solicitor and has written a large number of books on the subjects of Freemasonry and Christianity such as *La Metáfora Masónica, Razón y Sentido* (San Sebastián, 1999) and *Cristianismo Sin Embargo*, (Oviedo, 2011) as well as a series of works of fiction to cite some of his many books. He was the Grand Master of the Gran Logia Simbólica Española in 1997 and co-founded the lodge Manuel Iradier No.26 in 1993. Javier is a 33rd degree Freemason and a member of the Gran Logia Simbólica Española. His insight is particularly helpful given the fact that he was the president of CLIPSAS for a period of three years.

### Interview

**Dear Javier, thank you very much for talking to me today. Perhaps you could start by elaborating on your masonic journey so far?**

I approached Freemasonry when I was living and working in Bilbao in the legal profession. A colleague told me he was going to be initiated in a Masonic lodge and this whetted my appetite to discover more. I didn't know much about Freemasonry but it always attracted me. The mere fact that Franco, the Spanish dictator, hated it so much gave me the impression that Freemasonry had to be necessarily a good thing. But I did approach Freemasonry with a very superficial frame of mind I must confess. Thank God that Freemasonry happens to be something far more interesting and fascinating than I gave it credit for before joining. And this is why I have been in Freemasonry for thirty years. In 1981 when I joined I imagined Freemasonry to be a kind of freethinking athenaeum, a place where people debated and shared lectures and essays. But I soon discovered that Freemasonry is actually an initiatory tradition, an existential methodology and a philosophical fraternity. It is far more interesting than I initially expected it to be.

**What is Freemasonry for you then? What role does it play in your view? Is it an individual role of self-perfection or a social role?**

As an initiatory tradition Freemasonry has more of a sociable role than a social one: it is not a group of social activism. Freemasonry is an intellectual and moral tradition that employs a series of moral dramas in order to provoke in us a reflection on our existence and our human condition and it does so in an open, non-dogmatic way so that in the end each man and woman will be able to find their own particular answer to this quest in accordance with their biography, circumstances, personality, education and particular ideological and spiritual beliefs. In this sense Freemasonry is a method for the individual as it is a unique and personal path. Of course, all brothers and sisters will encourage and support each other but the task of 'building the self' is down to each individual Freemason.

**What is CLIPSAS? What function does it fulfil today?**

CLIPSAS is and was always a beautiful and ambitious project which simply has the aim of strengthening the chain of union between all the Grand Lodges and Grand Orients in the world regardless of their differences in method, approach, organisation and ritual considering that as there is a strong link uniting us at our core. At the turn of the century, in the year 2000's meeting in Athens, a symbolic city if there was ever one, as the representatives of all the Grand Lodges and Grand Orients we wanted to show the value and relevance of the 1962 Appeal of Strasbourg. We reached the conclusion that modern, speculative Freemasonry as we know it today was born in 1723 on the basis of the Anderson Constitutions with the objective of being a 'centre of union' between people who, were it not because of Freemasonry, would have never met. The Anderson Constitutions offered a new form of sociability to many people who were at the time divided by religion and politics but who had, unbeknownst to them, a shared ideal for improving humanity and from that ideal a new fraternity was developed. Anderson's Constitutions managed to gather what 'was dispersed' through the symbolic language of masonic ritual which allows us all to be united in spite of what may divide us. Paradoxically and rather unfortunately with time some divisions have crept into Freemasonry which makes a new understanding of what the 'centre of union' is indispensable. This is why the Appeal of Strasbourg was created in 1962: it is a document that ranks as highly as the Anderson Constitutions and which hopes to self-apply the original values that the Anderson Constitutions applied to the society of the eighteenth century, this is to create a centre of union between and Masonic Orders which would have never materialised had it not been for the Appeal of Strasbourg.

The Appeal of Strasbourg is founded on an absolute Freedom of Conscience. This principle when applied to Freemasonry means that every Freemason, each lodge and each Obedience are free to interpret individually and collectively the tradition and method of Freemasonry, either following a theist approach, a rationalistic one or understanding Freemasonry as an initiatory fraternity for men, women or mixed gender lodges. Freedom of Conscience as espoused by the Appeal of Strasburg is founded on the freedom that each masonic Grand Lodge or Grand Orient has to work the masonic method according to their own principles. There are however some common elements which admit of no compromise.

The Appeal of Strasbourg is the basis of CLIPSAS and attempts to establish a definition of what is a 'Just and Perfect Lodge', a definition that can be used as a common reference for all masonic Orders which are members of CLIPSAS and that can guarantee the commonalities existing between all the different traditions living side by side within modern Freemasonry. CLIPSAS is a platform that has been set up to foster good communication between all the member bodies and to provide a formative element. The advancement in new technologies and communication will allow CLIPSAS to have more success in fulfilling this role than previously. CLIPSAS can easily complement and support any bilateral relations between Masonic Orders and any masonic forums willing to participate. In the twenty-first century we must recognise the huge importance that CLIPSAS can play serving Freemasonry and the ideals of the Appeal of Strasbourg as a renovation of the moral and spiritual tradition inherent in the Anderson Constitutions.

**How about your particular experience as president of CLIPSAS?**

I was elected president of CLIPSAS in 1997. This was a period of crisis since the Grand Orient of France, one of the founding members, decided to resign from CLIPSAS. In spite of this set back we worked very hard to preserve both CLIPSAS and the Appeal since we believed in their importance on a moral, practical and also historical level. Fortunately the Grand Orient of France has reconsidered its decision and returned to CLIPSAS. I have great memories of my experience as president of CLIPSAS. In particular I remember the friendship and support of many dear brothers: Franco Franchi from the Gran Loggia d'Italia; Marc-Antoine Cauchie from the Grand Orient of Luxembourg; Eugenio de Oliveira from the Grand Orient of Portugal; Louis A. Daly from the Omega Grand Lodge of New York; Sergio Troncoso from the Grand Mixed Lodge of Chile; Maria Angela Alvarez from the SCM in Sao Paulo; Jefferson Isaac Joao Scheer from the Grand United Lodge of Paraná; Ivan Herrera from the Grand Lodge of North Colombia; the brethren from the Grand Liberal Lodge of Turkey and so many others.

The only bad memories I have are the ones derived from our lack of ability to be consistent with our ideals sometimes. Many Masonic Orders tend to prefer bilateral relations to multilateral ones which are much more difficult to negotiate.

What is most important in my view is that CLIPSAS, as the centre of union for Freemasonry, incorporates its definition of the requirements for a 'Just and Perfect Lodge' as a compulsory point of reference, as a new landmark which is more inclusive and open than the stagnant landmarks of the United Grand Lodge of England which no longer have the potential to embrace Freemasonry as a whole.

**What do you make of other Masonic forums such as SIMPA and CATENA?**

I think it is great that there are other platforms available so long as any other forums are always supportive of CLIPSAS so we do not lose direction and we can make the most of the Appeal of Strasbourg and CLIPSAS.

**What do you think of Masonic regularity and do you think that one day regular Freemasonry will recognise Liberal Freemasonry? Do you think CLIPSAS is still relevant today and has a part to play in this?**

We have to continue working and gradually expanding Masonic inter-visitation through CLIPSAS but without any anxiety or forcefulness, without seeing this as some kind of war of influences always trusting the moral and intellectual integrity of the Appeal of Strasbourg. We mustn't be disingenuous and realise that these changes are going to take time to come into effect. Let us make the most of what the Appeal and CLIPSAS has granted us so far. I believe that CLIPSAS is still relevant but more needs to be done; in my view CLIPSAS should ensure that all its member bodies include the Appeal of Strasbourg in their constitutions in order for the Appeal to become the new criteria for Masonic regularity.

**Is Freemasonry still relevant today? Why? What does the future hold for Freemasonry in your opinion?**

When we talk about Freemasonry we are really talking about two different things: one the one hand we are referring to the personal experience of each Freemason, this is our experience in lodge with our masonic brethren and our own work and on the other hand we are also referring to Freemasonry as the institution both national and international working to restore and strengthen the chain of union and which give our own tradition a face in the world. Freemasonry is relevant in the measure it remains faithful to its spiritual and philosophical essence. It will continue to be relevant so long as it keeps the masonic method alive with its precious working tools inviting us to question ourselves and to seek for the best possible version of ourselves. For me what is most important in Freemasonry is that personal and intimate experience. As an institution, Freemasonry is nothing more than an artefact, a structure with all its hierarchies and human vanities. Institutional Freemasonry exists and has value only as the support of that other personal and intimate Freemasonry to which we are all invited as unique human beings, men and women alike.

**Do you have any projects that you would care to share with us?**

Actually I do. The questions you have made in this interview have got me thinking. I am going to write a small essay in which I will discuss the relationship between the Anderson Constitutions of 1721 and 1723 and the Appeal of Strasbourg of 1962 on which CLIPSAS was founded.

**Always the indefatigable hard working writer Javier! Thank you very much for your time.**

# APPENDIX 3

## Interview with Julian Rees – Between Masonic Worlds

Julian Rees is a celebrated and much-loved Masonic author and Freemason. He was initiated into regular Freemasonry in 1968 from which he resigned in 2011 to join the British Federation of Le Droit Humain. He has written a number of books on the subject of Freemasonry and his perspective on Freemasonry as a method for spiritual improvement is fascinating and has inspired many people both in and outside of Freemasonry.

### Introduction

Julian Rees was born in London in 1936, the son of an Anglo-Catholic clergyman father and an American mother. He was brought up partly in London and partly in Dorset during the war, attended St Paul's School London from 1948 – 1954 and was called up into the Royal Army Education Corps for National Service in 1957. He served as Sergeant Instructor for three years mostly in Berlin where he met and subsequently married Arne Hubmann. After his army service, Julian followed a successful career in the textile industry. He was initiated in the Kirby Lodge no. 2818 under the United Grand Lodge of England in 1968, attending on a regular basis the Emulation Lodge of Improvement of which in time he became a member of the Precepting Committee, and of which body he is a holder of the coveted Silver Matchbox award for delivering a perfect ceremony from the Chair. In 1997 he assisted in the launch of the independent masonic quarterly magazine *Freemasonry Today* and under the editorship of Tobias Churton he wrote articles for that magazine. He later, under the editorship of Michael Baigent, became Deputy Editor. He has lectured to masonic lodges in France, Germany, Denmark, Norway, USA and Nigeria. He was invited by Lewis Masonic to write a replacement of the JSM Ward booklets in the three Craft degrees and this work appeared under the title *Making Light – a Handbook for Freemasons*. This was followed by four other works: *The Stairway of Freemasonry* (short talks for lodges); *So You Want to be a Freemason?; Tracing Boards of the Three Degrees in Craft Freemasonry Explained* and *Ornaments, Furniture and* Jewels. He was appointed Grand Pursuivant and later Junior Grand Deacon (active). He served as Master of Kirby Lodge in 1976 and again at the Centenary in 2000 and wrote the history of that Lodge. He also served as Master of the German-speaking Pilgrim Lodge no. 238, the Old Pauline Lodge no. 3969, the Canonbury Tower Lodge no. 9772 and as MEZ of the Grand Master's Chapter no. 1. He was a founder member and Secretary of The Cornerstone Society. He has been honoured by the Institut Maçonnique de France with the Ordre Maçonnique de Lafayette. In 2011, following the declaration in open Grand Lodge of the rejection of the spiritual pursuit of UGLE Freemasonry, he resigned from UGLE and joined the International Order of Freemasonry for Men and Women Le Droit Humain.

**Interview**

**Hello Julian and thank you very much for putting yourself forward for this interview. Yours has been undoubtedly a very busy and distinguished Masonic career (path?), would you care to elaborate on it?**

I would question the use of the word 'distinguished' but it has certainly been busy. It seems that almost since my initiation I have been deeply interested in the inner meaning of Freemasonry; as a young Master Mason I questioned some of the older Brethren about the meaning of the words in the Emulation Lectures, which seemed to me to point towards a vibrant and coherent spiritual content, but was advised by them to simply learn the words and not to worry too much about the meaning! From my early years I have been writing on Masonic topics, and once I had become a Past Master I found that Lodges and individual Brethren were interested in inviting me to give talks on what I was writing about. On one occasion I was invited to lecture to a very old and prestigious Lodge in New York. It was at the time when several US Grand Lodges were conducting what they called 'Grand Master's One-Day Classes' which were in fact occasions for initiating, passing and raising several hundred (even thousands) of men on one day in one place, and passing and raising them in the same weekend! I criticised this in my lecture and was cheered by the younger Masons. Back in England I wrote an article critical of this practice in the pages of *Freemasonry Today*. But my masonic activity, aside from ritual work in lodges, has centred on writing and lecturing.

**Your transition from Regular Freemasonry to Liberal Freemasonry is something that I find fascinating and that is extremely relevant to the subject matter of this book, would you mind sharing with us your experience in both Masonic worlds and the reasons of your resignation in the United Grand Lodge of England?**

We call it 'regular' Freemasonry, as that is the name by which the world at large knows it, but I dislike the term, as it implies that all other Freemasonry is then, by definition, 'irregular'. Consider for a moment that the vast majority of freemasons in France are not 'recognised' by the United Grand Lodge of England. Yet the masonic scene in France is alive and vibrant – alone in Europe, masonic membership in France is on the increase. One needs to consider that the majority of ritual work in all Obediences in France is centred on a secular spiritual pursuit. For years I worked away in Freemasonry, unaware that in France and other countries – including UK – there was something meaningful taking place. It is true that I had been asking questions about the deeper meaning in Freemasonry and more times than not running up against a brick wall, but gradually I began to meet with, and have conversations with, like-minded brethren in UGLE who, like me, were seeking something better, something more meaningful. The moment came when a group of us decided to found The Cornerstone Society, to explore the *real* meaning of Freemasonry, aside from the ever more elaborate regalia. The Cornerstone Society held conferences twice a year and we made great progress. But then the idea came to us of founding our own lodge, to practise in ritual what we had been talking about in conferences, and so the Canonbury Tower Lodge was formed, under the patronage of The Marquess of Northampton who, after the Consecration, became an ordinary member. At that time, Lord Northampton was Assistant Grand Master (later Pro-Grand Master) and so the Lodge had a certain standing in the eyes of senior UGLE freemasons. Yet it was still an oasis of meaning and spiritual content in a desert, a desert devoid, largely, of attempts to explore the universe and its meaning for humankind and, above all, the pursuit of self-knowledge. And, of course, UGLE still excluded women, whereas in France and other countries women were already an integral part in the search for the perfection of humanity. This is not to say that there are no in 'regular' Freemasonry who have not seen the Light – there are many, and many are still good friends of mine, but their esoteric activities are strictly curtailed – there is a lodge which seeks to follow a more esoteric path, but which is more or less regularly brought to heel. Realising that esoteric pursuits were not making progress in UGLE, I began to make contacts with the International Order of Freemasonry for Men and Women Le Droit Humain, an Obedience spread over the globe. I immediately found that their ritual pursuit accorded with my own view of what Freemasonry should be, and of course I found that most attractive. For me then, the breaking point came when the Deputy Grand Master declared in open Grand Lodge in 2011 that UGLE Freemasonry did not 'deal in spirituality'. Such a pronouncement, made *ex cathedra* as it was, made it quite clear to me that UGLE was not the place for me and accordingly I resigned and applied to join Le Droit Humain. The break was not painless. Those who imagine it to be so do not understand what is involved. But in the end, the enormous benefits outweighed what I was giving up. I now count myself fortunate to have found my true Masonic home, and I witness almost daily other UGLE members making the same journey.

**What is Freemasonry for you? Do you think it is a method for personal improvement, a spiritual path or do you think it should play a part in the social and political affairs of the world?**

To take your last point first, I do not believe that Freemasonry should ever be involved in social and political affairs. I know that many Obediences in other parts of the world do so, but for me that detracts from the main purpose of, Freemasonry – a non-religious, secular spiritual pursuit. Everywhere, the symbolism points towards self-improvement, self-perfection, knowledge of the spirit – the point within a circle; Jacob's ladder; the winding staircase; working on the rough ashlar to make it perfect; I could go on. Yet many branches of Freemasonry wilfully ignore this all-important aspect.

In earlier centuries adherence in the western world to religion supplied that all-important spiritual nourishment we all need, but religious observance has declined, in the 20th and 21st centuries very rapidly. Material pursuits and the satisfying of our sensual appetites have become all-pervading.

Following up from the previous question, do you think that Freemasonry has a role to play in the world at large today?

I am quite sure that the present-day lack of a satisfactory spiritual pursuit is leading to degeneration in society. We care less than we did in previous centuries, less about ourselves and through that less about our fellow human beings. How often do we perceive in others a lack of self-worth? Psychoanalysts will attest to this. Of course there are shining examples of adherence to a spiritual path – Pope Francis is a powerful example of such. So yes, I do feel that Liberal, non-dogmatic Freemasonry has a role to play, and it is up to us to make it more widely known.

**What do you think the future holds for Freemasonry?**

I am afraid that dogmatic Freemasonry may continue to decline, but I believe this decline will be accompanied by a resurgence in attention to all kinds of spiritual pursuits, chief amongst these a resurgence of Liberal, non-dogmatic Freemasonry. The signs are there. We are approaching a true new age. I am quite upbeat about this.

**Do you think that we will see one day regular Freemasonry recognising at institutional level other Obediences/Orders and even allowing inter-visitation?**

Yes. The largest Masonic Obedience in France now admits women, so it cannot be long now before UGLE does the same. Liberal Freemasonry recognises members from regular Obediences – a shining example of brotherhood and compassion which is waiting to be reciprocated.

**Do you have any projects in the way of books or talks you would like to share with us?**

I do not have any specific projects on the drawing board, although I will shortly be publishing a PowerPoint presentation entitled *The Power of Allegory* I gave in Denmark recently, and the British Federation will shortly be publishing a video *Today's Freemasonry for Men and Women* which some of us have been working on.

**Thank you very much for your time Julian.**
Thank you. London, November 2017

# APPENDIX 4

**Interview with Philippe Bodhuin from the Grand Orient of France**

Philippe is a member of the Grand Orient of France and a prominent member of their lodge Freedom of Conscience which works in the United Kingdom.

Philippe's Masonic curriculum is impressive:

Worshipful Master of the lodge « Freedom of Conscience » in the Orient of LONDON.

Former Grand Officer of the Order Council of Le Grand Orient de France (2007-2010)

Grand Orator (Lecturer) 2009-2010

Honorary member of the Worshipful Lodge « Tricolor N°1 » of the Grand Orient of Ireland.

Bond Guarantor between GODF and Grand Orient of Ireland and Grand Loge of Malta.

Higher Degrees AASR: 32° degree, Member of the Consistory in Lille (France), Aeropagus, Chapter and Perfection Lodge in Dunkerque and Calais.

Mark Masonry: Mark Master Mason, member of Keystone Mark Lodge N°5 of the Grand Orient of Ireland.

**When and why did you knock on the door of the lodge? When and why did you solicit to be admitted into the mysteries and privileges of Freemasonry?**

I was 38 when I knocked on the door of the Worshipful Lodge Les 5 Etoiles (the 5 stars) in France. I was interested in symbolism (having approached symbolism during my studies, but only through mythology or psychoanalysis). Some friends told me I would find my way in Freemasonry and amongst the free and good people who make up its lodges. I was not very fond of being a member of large groups such as the Lion's Club but I was surprised by the way I immediately found my place in Freemasonry. I met many interesting people (men and women) with whom I quickly developed fraternal bonds, and I also really appreciated the exchanges on philosophical, social and symbolical topics.

**Tell us a bit about yourself.**

My childhood was very happy and my parents taught my siblings and me to be independent and responsible. We were also very close to Anglo-Saxon culture, because of the English origins of my father's family. Therefore, we developed a very strong interest in travel and in the acquisition of other languages as well as a respect and admiration for other cultures. I also did a lot of sport and practised fencing at an international level, which gave me the opportunity to meet many people of other countries, and to travel, too.

I have always been a good student and when I was 17 years old just before going to the University, I took one year off and travelled through France, Germany, Britain, Belgium and the Netherlands. One of my best experiences was to attend the 1970 Isle of Wight Music festival. Music and concerts (Classical, Opera, but also Rock and Heavy Metal) have always been important to me.

I had a very keen interest in Latin, Greek, Literature and Philosophy and the study of Classics, and obtained a Master's degree, but I realized very soon that I was not motivated in becoming a teacher. Therefore I also started my studies in Psychology, specialising in social psychology and psycho-sociology (study of Groups and organisations). This led me to the profession of Human Resources Management Consultant, which I have been practising for the last 35 years, as a freelance consultant.

I have never been a religious man, but I think atheists or agnostics can have an interest in the spiritualistic dimension. I think that if we do not have faith in some supreme being, we can believe in the humanistic ideals, and feel some kind of responsibility towards all human beings. Defining yourself like a citizen of the world means that you believe in what the Greeks (Aristoteles) called 'kosmos' which means the order of the world.

Freemasonry was a great discovery in that sense, and I took many offices and roles in the functioning of Le Grand Orient de France (Grand Officer from 2007 to 2010), and in several lodges, rites and degrees. An important event was the creation of a GODF English-speaking Lodge in London (the Worshipful Lodge Freedom of Conscience), in which sisters and brothers of several nationalities (UK, Belgium, France, Ireland, Italy, Spain, Grenada, Turkey etc.) work together with great enthusiasm. This also gave me the opportunity to help some Irish Brothers in creating the Grand Orient of Ireland by consecrating their first Lodge in Killarney, in the name of Le Grand Orient de France, and to become a member of two of their Lodges. Another great experience was to get in touch with the Bros. of the Grand Lodge of Malta, and to help them establish a treaty of amity with Le Grand Orient de France. In 2013, the Order Council appointed me as Bond Guarantor between GODF, Grand Orient of Ireland, Grand Lodge of Malta and Lodges of England.

**What impression did your initiation leave in you?**

The journeys or the obscurity did not really impress me, but I really felt the meaning of the ritual like a real teaching about myself. On the other hand, I was amazed how confident I was towards people I did not know. The most impressive part for me was the end of the meeting, when all Sisters and Brethren approached me and gave me the fraternal triple hug. Then I felt what the word fraternity meant.

**What do you think of death?**

I think death is the end of life, and being an atheist, I do not think there is something afterwards (except some kind of biological return to Mother Nature). This only means that our only goal should be to make a success in every part of our lives. Trying to be happy in life and good to others is enough to fulfil a lifetime. Does not mean that it is easy to do…

**What are your values, ideals and dreams?**

Freedom of thought and respect for all human beings. I think we are responsible of what we do, but also mostly responsible for what happens to us. The best definition of freedom is the one in the 1948 Human rights declaration: "Freedom consists in doing everything that does not do any harm to anyone."

An ideal (or a dream) would be to see people ceasing to fear or envy others. I love Isaac Newton's sentence: "Men build too many walls and not enough bridges."

**What are your most happy achievements in life and how do you see the future?**

I am not sure I am the best judge of it, but I think that my partner Evelyn and I have well raised our two children, and helped them in getting the necessary qualities and knowledge to succeed in life. We have always been in harmony with the proverb "The only things you can give to your children are roots and wings".

I also think that I have always done my job well, to the best of my abilities. I did not make a lot of money, but as a freelance consultant, I made a living and managed to have a comfortable life and I think and hope that I have been helpful to my clients and students. Besides, I always managed to save time for living my passions and interest (Sport, culture and Freemasonry), and for my family and friends.

The most important problems faced by humanity today are:

One: the resurgence of religious bigotry that carries the misunderstanding of the universal message of religion (which is in my view something like "Love each other"). This can release the darkest parts of the human nature (I mean fear, greed and search of power), and lead to war, terrorism and/or fascism ("Gott mit uns"!).

Two: the leaders of political and/or economic organizations (with the support of the majority of the voters/consumers), are incapable to do their job for the benefit of the whole humanity. This leads to communitarian or nationalist attitudes, or to the confiscation of resources for the benefit of a privileged minority of people.

**Have you travelled? What countries have you seen? What experience have you gained from your travels?**

I have travelled a lot and seen France, Switzerland, Ireland, Belgium, Luxembourg, the Netherlands, Spain, Germany, Malta, Canada and Tunisia. I lived in England and in the United States for a few months, and stayed a few weeks in Morocco and Algeria for work. In all my travels, I have always tried to meet people and get to know them and their customs. I think it brings you many friends, but it also teaches you tolerance and opens your mind.

Travelling has allowed me to learn and improve my English, German and Spanish. Speaking several foreign languages is a great privilege and this should be a priority in the education of children. This is the only way to get in touch with foreign people, to understand them and to create real bonds with them.

I wish I had travelled more and further (Asia, Australia…), but I hope I will be able to do so in the future.

**Have you experienced dark moments in your life?**

My partner Evelyn (we have never been married, but live together since 1972 and have had two children who are now 26 and 31) had to face several problems like the untimely deaths of her father and a younger brother, and 2 severe breast cancers. All that led her to chronical neurotic depression for about 20 years now. Life has not always been easy, but we have always tried to handle the difficult moments the best we could.

In 2013, I was diagnosed with chronic leukaemia. The doctors finally found the right treatment and I am all right now (though I will never completely recover). In the meantime, we had to face the possibility of death, and I discovered myself serene and confident, and relatively fearless. It did not change my position of being a strict non-believer.

**What do you hope from life?**

I hope that the years to come will allow me to keep discovering new knowledge, new people and new parts of the world. I totally agree with the Nietzsche's conceptions of "Amor fati" and "Eternal recurrence". Until the end, "say yes to life!"

**What motivates you?**

First of all, love and fraternity. We do not exist without the others, and the ultimate mirror is the other's eyes. That does not mean that you must forge your life and acts in order to give a good image of yourself, but that you only will get to know who you really are in the thousands of mirrors of the other's eyes. Each of them reflecting a part of the truth about you, but also some distortion. And you are the only one capable of sorting out the truth out of these two polarities.

**What makes you feel good, where do you find solace in life?**

The moments of happiness shared with family and friends, of course!
The moments where you have the feeling of discovering something new (in a book or in watching a play or attending a concert).
There are some (rare) moments of meditation and/or "egregore" (some kind of collective spirit) during the work in a masonic Lodge. For most Masons, these are probably prayers, but (as we have no prayers in our Lodges) it is also a deep feeling of being together in a sacred space, and feeling the same elevation of thought.

# APPENDIX 5

## Interview with Lorena Clara: The female perspective

Lorena was born in Valencia in 1980 and read history and archaeology at university. She started working for Hewlett Packard in the customer service department and was promoted to supervisor in their project management department. She obtained a scholarship with the Erasmus Mundus Programme during the last year of her degree and relocated to Genoa in Northern Italy where she completed her studies. Upon her return to Spain, Lorena worked in five successive archaeological projects in the 'Cova del Bolomor' in Spain, a very important Palaeolithic archaeological site due to the evidence of early controlled use of fire technology found on the site. She didn't remain in this field of work and continued working for Hewlett Packard.

Lorena loves reading and has a great interest in philosophy as well as in Freemasonry, her beloved archaeology and new technologies. She joined the Spanish Federation of Le Droit Humain in 2011 and is an active member in two lodges: Alba de Levante in the Orient of Valencia and Migdia in the Orient of Castellón.

**Dear Lorena, when did you become a Freemason and why?**

I was initiated in 2011 in the lodge Alba de Levante in the Orient of Valencia, one of the lodges in the Spanish Federation of Le Droit Humain which has managed to work without interruption since its foundation although I wasn't aware of the fact at the time.

It is difficult to pinpoint what exactly brought me to Freemasonry; I think my decision to join was more instinctual than rational. Freemasonry and its values had always fascinated me but I always thought that women couldn't be admitted so I never considered joining which made me lose interest in the topic. I was always interested in symbolism and in the subject of spirituality. When I was 30 years old I went through a process of introspection and soul searching and started to ponder about the meaning of life and what had been my contribution to the world and all the sort of things that usually come with what was an early onset of middle life crisis. Surfing the web one day I discovered the page of the Spanish Federation and this was the first time I realized that mixed gender Freemasonry existed. This renewed my interest in the subject and I started to read on it and realised that the values of Freemasonry as embodied in the triad Freedom, Equality and Fraternity resonated with my own. I do believe that the perfection of humanity starts first on an individual and personal level. And I have always believed that the best way to change the world is to first change oneself in order to become a reference and model for others. The fact that Freemasonry offers exactly that, a chance for self-improvement, made me want to join.

**What does it mean to you to be a woman and a Freemason?**

I think that the fact that I am a woman doesn't change anything. I have a very personal view on what Freemasonry means of course but I don't think that being a woman informs that view because I believe that each Freemason has his or her own view on the fraternity and that their particular understanding of Freemasonry is related to their own life experiences, their personal issues, their interest in learning, their commitment and their determination to overcome obstacles in order to better themselves. There are as many ways of understanding Freemasonry as there are, men and women alike, and this is so because the degrees worked in Freemasonry have such a profound impact on the candidates. This is why their experience is unique and because of this Freemasonry means different things to different people.

As a woman I am indebted to women like Maria Deraismes thanks to whom today I can call myself a Freemason. I am equally grateful to all the Brothers and Sisters who supported Maria Deraismes in spite of the opposition they encountered at the time when the Order was founded (Le Droit Humain). And of course, I am also thankful to all Brothers from other Orders, regular ones included, who consider me a Freemason. To be honest even though regular Freemasonry doesn't consider our Order masonic, I have yet to meet a regular Freemason who hasn't recognised me as a Freemason and I know many since we share one of the Temples in Valencia. It is interesting to note that the Masters of regular lodges and our own who sometimes are women have to meet to make decisions on administrative matters related to the shared Temple and facilities and there are never any issues or conflicts in spite of the obligations made by regular about not having contact with irregular freemasons. I find all this incongruent.

I believe that women will eventually be accepted in regular Freemasonry as a matter of course. I perfectly understand that Freemasonry was only for men in its origins as it was a product of its time. The main requisite for admission is 'Being free and of good report' and women were neither in those days. A woman was under the tutelage of her father, husband or brother and had no rights so I can understand that women were not accepted at the time. But as women's rights have developed and society has become freer and more egalitarian it is only natural that women can now be initiated into Freemasonry. It simply cannot be any other way. Some masonic orders have decided to create mixed gender lodges and others have given each lodge the freedom to make a decision on the matter of accepting women or not. For me personally Freemasonry doesn't have any meaning if it's exclusively male or female: the lodge is like a microcosm, a miniature reflection of society at large where the same problems and conflicts take place on a smaller scale and where these issues are resolved or at least attempted to be resolved through the application of the masonic triad of freedom, equality and fraternity. And trying to see the world through these ideals can only have a positive impact. Can you imagine what the world would look like if these values were practised by everyone? It would be a better place. If the lodge is this microcosm, a slice of humanity, how can it then exclude women? A lodge cannot work towards the perfection of humanity if it excludes women; only to half of humanity. You cannot study and deepen your understanding of concepts such as the Great Architect of the Universe, the One or the Supreme Being if you are ignoring half of the human race.

Reformulating your question, what does it mean for me to be a Freemason as a human being, as a person? I would say that it means making a conscious effort to ensure that my thoughts, words and actions are reflecting masonic ideals. If you believe in Equality then you cannot put yourself above others. If you believe in Freedom you will respect other people's freedom while asserting your own. If you believe in Fraternity you won't merely treat others like equals but as brothers or sisters in your shared humanity regardless of how different from you they may appear to be. This is not easy nor it's always possible but for me, as a Freemason, this way of thinking always brings me 'to order' and forces me to keep my thoughts and actions in check and to correct them when required.

Being a Freemason also means that I must be more tolerant and understanding. Freemasonry asks us to acquire self-knowledge and if we put in that effort to know ourselves we are indirectly making an effort to know our fellow human beings too.

**How is Freemasonry viewed in Spain nowadays?**

There are many prejudices against it and there is also a lot of ignorance about the fraternity. Freemasonry completely disappeared in Spain during General Franco's dictatorship and were prosecuted during this period. Very few brothers and sisters survived and many had to seek refuge abroad. Freemasonry was banned for more than 40 years and was only legalised in 1979.

The most common reactions I find when the subject of Freemasonry is broached are as follows:

- Some do not want to declare publicly their membership, mainly because they are afraid that the institution might suffer again from government prosecution or because it might affect their career and job prospects. This fear is also prevalent among family members when you approach them and tell them you intend to join Freemasonry.

- There is always the fear of Freemasonry being a sect and this is due to the secretive aspects of the rituals and a lack of understanding of its aims and objectives.

- Total and utter ignorance of what Freemasonry is or if it even exists. I see this mainly among young people who will see the compass and square symbol and think nothing of it.

Many Spanish brethren I know don't declare their membership and do not want to feature in any photographs of public events in order to avoid being recognised. Many haven't even disclosed their membership to their families because it would cause them problems. It took me three years to tell my family and only my partner knew at the time I was a Freemason. After spending an hour discussing my masonic membership with my mother she replied: 'Since you haven't changed in these past three years then I suppose I have nothing to worry about'. I believe that my mother's main concern was that I was involved with a sect.

**What do you remember most of your initiation?**

I have very fond memories of that day, I remember being very nervous and feeling uncertainty. I had no idea of what was in store although a lot of initiates do read the rituals prior to being initiated. I chose not to because nowadays you can find plenty of information on the internet, some good and some bad but at the time I lacked the basic knowledge to make an informed decision so I chose not to read up on the subject and to allow my intuition to guide me.

My initiation made a profound impact on me but it is difficult to put into words as this is something which must be experienced. This is what the masonic secret really is: you can read the ritual books but you will only understand what the degrees are when you experience them. In fact I think that reading the ritual book before experiencing it conditions our subsequent experience and impedes us from 'feeling' it as it was meant to be felt and experienced. We could compare this to watching a film in its entirety, with its soundtrack, photography, storyline and so on. If we read the script before watching the film when we do we will lose out. We won't feel the thrill and the emotion of watching that film for the first time and we will not fully enjoy the whole experience. To read the ritual before going through the degree is, in my opinion, to miss the secret that is imparted in that degree. For that reason I don't want to elaborate on my initiation as this would be a spoiler for others wishing to go through this experience. It was a very special and important moment in my life which made me face up to some very deep seated fears.

**What would you like to share with us about your Order, the Spanish Federation of Le Droit Humain? I know that you have been a regular at many of the convents of the Spanish Federation what were your experiences there?**

The Spanish Federation is a very new organisation if compared to the French or the Belgian Federations. It is also a small Federation although it has experienced a significant growth in terms of lodges. I co-founded the lodge Migdia in the Orient of Castellón in 2015 for example. I am still an active member of this lodge and my mother lodge in Valencia.

I have attended the convents of the Spanish Federation in the Orient of Madrid which normally take place every year over a weekend in September. I have taken part in these convents as a representative of my lodge and also as an assistant. It is a very gratifying experience because it is a great opportunity to meet brothers and sisters from all over Spain and to learn how the federation is administered. But most importantly one can feel the fraternal aspect of Freemasonry in a very moving way. Administrative matters are discussed and of course these aren't as exciting as the discussions on symbolism and ritual. It is a wonderful thing to be able to partake of that fraternal spirit with people you may have just met, something that isn't possible in our day-to-day lives.

What has your experience as Secretary of your lodge been like during these past years?

My first appointment in that office was as assistant secretary. I was only a Fellow Craft at the time. By the time I was raised to the degree of Master Mason I was familiar enough with the duties of that office to feel confident to take it on and I was duly installed as Secretary. I have been Secretary of my mother lodge in Valencia for three consecutive years and I am also Secretary of the lodge Migdia since its foundation.

The office of lodge Secretary is probably one of the busiest ones, especially when you are doing it in two lodges. It is the only office, aside from the one of Worshipful Master, which requires daily or at the very least weekly attention. Through this office one can learn very well the general rules and regulations of the Order and also the ritual since for almost every ceremony the input of the Secretary is usually required. This is an office that requires discretion above all else. As the secretary one is in constant and direct contact with the Worshipful Master which is another opportunity to learn about the workings of the lodge and Freemasonry in general.

**Do you think that Freemasonry still has a part to play in the world today? What does the future hold for Freemasonry?**

For me Freemasonry is a personal path of self-improvement which creates better people and a better world. In that sense I believe that Freemasonry has a very important part to play in the world. And this is very true today when we see that many of the values, certainties and ideals of the world are either in crisis or being questioned.

However, and this is my personal opinion with which I am sure many of my brothers and sisters will disagree, I do not believe that the role of Freemasonry lies in public rallies and demonstrations where we demand things which have nothing to do with Freemasonry and we shouldn't be doing politics instead of practising Freemasonry. must perfect themselves in their lodges so that they can then share their values from other platforms as individuals be it political platforms, lobbies or NGOs.

# BIBLIOGRAPHY

Alberdi, J *Nosotros y la Crisis* Cultura Masonica Revista de Francmasoneria Editorial Masonica Es (Spain,January 2013)

Béresniak,, A *Daniel Béresniak,, mi padre, un hermano* Cultura Masonica Revista de Francmasoneria Editorial Masonica Es (Spain 2014).

Béresniak,, D *Symbols of Freemasonry (Beliefs and Symbols)*.Assouline,(France. October 2000).

Benimelli, J A Masoneria, Iglesia, *Revolucion e Independencia. Pontificia Universidad* Javeriana, (Bogota, Colombia 2015)

Callaey, R E *El Mito de la Revolucion Masonica* Ediciones Nowtilus, S.L. (Madrid, April 2007).

Cobos, J L *La Vida, un recorrido lleno de recovecos* Cultura Masonica Revista de Francmasoneria Editorial Masonica Es (Spain 2014).

Cooper L.D. R, *Cracking the Freemason's Code* (Random House Books, 2007).

Conner, M *Voices of Gnosticism* Bardic Press, (Dublin, November 2010)

Dachez, R & Bauer A, *Freemasonry: a French view* Westphalia Press, France, June 2013 (All rights reserved Policy Studies Organisation 2015)

Keghel, A, *Las Incursiones del Grand Oriente de Francia en la Politica Francesa* Cultura Masonica Revista de Francmasoneria Editorial Masonica Es, (Spain, July 2015).

Diaz, V *El Futuro de la Masoneria* Cultura Masonica Revista de Francmasoneria Editorial Masonica Es, (Spain, January 2016).

Ferrer Benimeli, J A *Masoneria, Iglesia, Revolucion e Independencia* Editorial Pontificia universidad Javeriana, (Bogota -Colombia January 2015).

Faulks P & Cooper L.D R *The Masonic Magician: The Life and Death of Count Cagliostro and his Egyptian Rite* Watkins Publishing, (London, September 2008).

Harrison, D *The Genesis of Freemasonry* Lewis Masonic, (London November 2014).

Hamill, J *The History of English Freemasonry* Lewis Masonic, (London 1994).

Keghel, A *La Masoneria: una perspectiva geopolítica* EntreAcacias, S.L. (Oviedo- Spain September 2013).

MacNulty W.K *Freemasonry, Secrets, Symbols, Significance* Thames and Hudson Ltd; 01 edition (6 Nov. 2006)

Michel Herrera, *Las Mujeres en el Gran Oriente de Francia entraron sin invitación ni alfombra roja* Cultura Masonica Revista de Francmasoneria Editorial Masonica Es, (Spain, July 2015).

Michel Herrera, I *'El Dialogo con Olivia Chaumont'* Cultura Masonica issue 15, Editorial Masonica Es, Asturias (Spain, 2013).

Mendez –Trelles, I *Textos Fundamentales de la Masoneria* Masonica Es (Spain, February 2002)

Otaola, J *La Ilustracion Escarmentada* Cultura Masonica Revista de Francmasoneria Editorial Masonica Es (Spain, April 2016).

Otaola, J *El Rito Escoces y la Metafora Caballeresca* Cultura Masonica Revista de Francmasoneria Editorial Masonica Es (Spain, October 2011)

Sickels, D *General Ahiman Rezon* independently published (1 Nov. 2017)

Var, J F *Jean Baptiste Willermoz: su obra* Editorial EntreAcacias S.L. (Spain, 2013)

Wilmshurst C.W *The Meaning of Freemasonry* Gramercy, United States, (December 1995).

Wilmshurst W.L, *The Meaning of Masonry*, Lund, Humphris & Co; W.Rider & Son, (London 1922).

# ONLINE RESOURCES

The Internet Archive https://archive.org/about/ (Text of the Matthew Cooke Manuscript)

Catena https://www.catena.org/ (International Masonic Union)

Clipsas http://clipsas.news/?lang=en (Center Of Liaison and Information of Masonic Powers Signatories Strasbourg Appeal)

Diaz, V *Life and work of Daniel Béresniak,, a great Master Mason*, Cultura Masonica issue 16, Asturias

http://www.elcentrodelaunionescocesa.org/es/inicio/8-cates/articulos/12-xv-aniversario-de-la-logia-masonica-el-centro-de-la-union-escocesa

El Centro de la Union Escocesa ,http://www.elcentrodelaunionescocesa.org/en/

(Lodge belonging to the Grand Lodge of France working in Barcelona)

British Federation of Le Droit Humain: http://www.Freemasonryformenandwomen.co.uk

The Cooke Manuscript: https://archive.org/stream/The_Cooke_Manuscript_1450/The Cooke_Manuscript_1450_djvu.txt

Le Droit Humain International: https://droit-humain.org/web/

Masonic lectures are known in English as Pieces of Architecture, Planches in French and Planchas in Spanish.

Masoneria y Politica, Cultura Masonica Editorial Masonica, Asturias (Spain) 2013 https://www.catena.org/about-catena/basic-principles/

Le Grand Orient de France: http://www.godf.org/

The Grande Loge de France: https://www.gldf.org/

The Grand Symbolic Spanish Lodge: https://glse.org/

The Grand Lodge of Italy: http://www.granloggia.it/

The United Grand Lodge of England: http://www.ugle.o

Printed in Great Britain
by Amazon